Images of
BRADMAN

Above: Sir Donald Bradman, AC, and Lady Jessie Bradman in their Adelaide home, 1993.

Right: This is Sir Donald Bradman's favourite photograph of himself, taken during his world-record innings of 452 not out for NSW against Queensland at the Sydney Cricket Ground in 1929-1930. More than any other, it demonstrates the agility, power and artistry of the greatest batsman the world has ever seen.

Previous page: Bradman, 1936.

Images of
BRADMAN

Rare and famous photographs of a cricket legend

With special inclusions from Sir Donald Bradman's private collection

Edited by
Peter Allen & James Kemsley

THE BRADMAN MUSEUM

BOWRAL

Contents

THE BRADMAN ERA

Above left to right: Bradman 1916, 1930, 1950, 1990.

Foreword

by Richie Benaud

I can't recall if, the first time I ever saw Don Bradman play cricket, he touched a ball in the field. Probably he did, but, as one of a Saturday crowd of 30,400 in January,1940, my eyes were firmly fixed on the almost inconspicuous figure of Clarrie Grimmett who demolished Stan McCabe's New South Wales team by taking 6/118. At the close of play "Ginty" Lush had two of the South Australian wickets and Bradman had survived. I went home to practise leg breaks and on the Monday - no Sunday play in those distant days - Bill O'Reilly had Bradman lbw with a "googly" for 39.

There were 24,317 spectators at the SCG on the Monday, in keeping with the fact that when Bradman batted, on weekdays, working days or holidays, attendances almost doubled. I didn't say, as Don did to his father when he first savoured a match on the SCG, that I would never be satisfied until I played on the great ground, but later I did make my first-class and then my Test debut there.

Bradman retired the season I started, 1948-1949. Having a beer with Keith Miller after play one evening at the SCG, I offered the thought that of all the things which had happened to me, this was one of the saddest, that I never had the chance to bowl at him. Miller said nothing for a while, then suggested, in as nice a way as possible, that I might have had a lucky break!

There are many statistical books about Bradman, as there should be because he was the greatest. There are biographies, several of them, and he has written some excellent books; his *Art of Cricket* remains a classic. It should be compulsory reading for all coaches who preach complication rather than simplification in the game. Through all this literature, and now a variety of sound tapes and videotapes, a picture of Bradman has emerged for posterity, and it will be added to in splendid fashion by this publication. Having never bowled at him, and having watched him only in 1940 in the one match and then in 1946-1948, I never cease to wonder at the fact that he was so much better than anyone else.

We know that every top-class Test squad generally has in it one great player, and there are, say, four very good players, three good ones, two average and a couple who will always be fighting for a place. When you have two great players then you really do have a winning chance. When Australia had Bradman it was a different matter again.

A glance at the Australian first-class run-makers over a period of 60 years leaves The Don with more runs than anyone else at almost double the average and in ridiculously fewer matches. Greg Chappell was a great batsman, Neil Harvey was the most difficult Australian batsman I ever bowled against. They made 74 and 67 first-class centuries respectively against Bradman's 117. It is significant that when the modern-day players espouse the fact that cricketers today are as good as in every other era, which they certainly are, they always except Bradman.

One of the most startling and most talked-about statistics Channel Nine and BBC cricket producers put on the screen is the one relating to Highest Test Aggregates. From 52 Tests and 80 innings he was a whisker away from 7000 runs and it is the ultimate irony that soon, with the amount of Test cricket played around the world these days, Bradman's name will be squeezed onto page two of the Aggregates. Perhaps a page to himself might be more appropriate! Even 46 years after he retired from Test cricket the search for a batting star is only associated with his name, "Another Bradman".

With a photographic book which covers a subject's early life, and then concludes with the end of his playing career, there is not a great deal of scope for details about administrative work, or what kind of a cricket brain was brought to bear on Australian cricket. I was fortunate that my period of captaincy coincided with Bradman's tenure as Chairman of Selectors, with Jack Ryder and Dudley Seddon as the other two committee members. They were the best selectors I ever saw, thorough, consistently aggressive with their attitude to selections and thoughts on the game, and approachable.

I had captained Australia in the series against England in 1958-1959, and then in India and Pakistan in 1959-1960, but although there was great enthusiasm over beating England, the general standard of cricket around the country had not boosted attendances.

When we came to the series against the West Indies in 1960-1961, I had to pass a fitness test on the Thursday in

Brisbane before the selectors would allow me to play, and then The Don asked if he could address our team meeting that night. I said it was okay with me, but that I would come back to him after I had ensured it was all right with the team. I had no idea what he wanted to say. It was a message to every player in the side that the selectors would be looking in kindly fashion on players who played aggressively, who thought about the people paying their money at the turnstiles, who made the game attractive, and who won doing those things. They would look less kindly on those who treated the Australia-West Indies series as 25 days of boring attrition.

There were only 4100 spectators at the "Gabba" on the final day when the Test was tied and at tea Australia needed 123 to win, I was batting with Alan Davidson, we had four wickets in hand and two hours to play; in those days there was no set number of overs in the last hour.

Don came to the dressing-room, pouring himself a cup of tea, sat down alongside me on the bench outside the room and asked: "What are the tactics?" "We're going for a win," I replied. "I'm pleased to hear it," he said, looking straight ahead. The chat from the Chairman of Selectors the evening prior to the Test had a profound effect on cricket in Australia that afternoon and in the three years which followed.

Sir Donald once asked me if there was anything I particularly wanted by way of selection for the next Test. I said, "Yes," and nominated a bowler who, at the time, was not in a Sheffield Shield team. He said: "Okay, I'll tell the others, but don't hold your breath." He was right. I was lucky to have had him as Chairman and very fortunate to have been captain when the selection committee consisted of three people who served Australian cricket so well.

Images of Bradman captures some delightful aspects of his cricketing life and his life with Lady Bradman; Jessie has always been, and is, a star. The book underlines the enormous effect Bradman had on the game of cricket, confirms that the way is open in Australia for every young cricketer to play for his country and reminds us that a new and reprehensible form of attack was used to curb his batting genius, and that this also dramatically affected his team-mates.

The photographs, taken as far back as 86 years ago, are beautifully enhanced by modern methods because in this wonderful computer age anything is possible. Except, it seems, the matching of Bradman as a cricketer and the breaking of Don Bradman's records.

Benaud and Bradman, 1961.

Introduction

Wherever cricket is played, Sir Donald Bradman is, and will always remain, a legend. He was the most devastating batsman the world has ever seen. Many have sought to inherit his mantle. So far, all have failed. Some day, someone may succeed in bettering his amazing performances with the bat. But even if they do, there will still only ever be one Bradman. He was of an era and we will never see his like again.

When he retired as a player from the game he loved so much in 1949 he left behind a huge void. He also left behind a batting record far exceeding any other. But his most enduring legacy of all was the influence he exerted on the game over two decades and the inspiration he endowed on whole generations of future cricketers right around the world.

Time has enhanced rather than diminished his greatness. In the more than 45 years since he last graced the first-class arena some marvellous cricketers have emerged to enthral and entertain. Yet, the name Bradman remains supreme and, indeed, has become synonymous with excellence of performance of a rare and special kind.

The great English cricket writer, Sir Neville Cardus, unhesitatingly wrote of Bradman as the greatest cricketer the world has ever seen, a sentiment echoed over the decades by players and commentators alike. When Bradman retired, another great British writer, R.C. Robertson-Glasgow, recorded in *Wisden Cricketers' Almanack*: "Don Bradman will bat no more against England, and two contrary feelings dispute within us: relief, that our bowlers will no longer be oppressed by this phenomenon; regret, that a miracle has been removed from among us. So must ancient Italy have felt when she heard of the death of Hannibal." Writing in the London *Observer* in 1948, he said Bradman's figures were unanswerable when it came to comparing the all-time greats. He said: "You can't answer them. They don't speak. They exist; and will exist; a monument more enduring than bronze."

Like many youngsters in the immediate post World War II era, I grew up on a diet of boyhood cricket heroes: Bradman, Lindwall, Miller, Morris, Hassett and the rest. While denied the pleasure of watching Bradman bat, I was fortunate enough to at least experience a fleeting touch of his fame by sneaking out of bed in the dead of night to listen to his run-scoring deeds come crackling over the radio air waves from England during the 1948 tour. Those precious sounds, the ebb and flow of far-off English voices and the crescendo of the crowd as Bradman and Morris won a famous victory in the Fourth Test, remain forever etched in the memory.

We feasted too on the Bradman boyhood legend: how he spent hours hitting a golf ball against a tankstand, a classic story of a simple country boy's rise to stardom that fired hopes and visions of greatness in every lad old enough to pick up a cricket bat.

Those simplistic images remained for years. But, as I was to discover, the Bradman legend is a far more complex and fascinating story. Many of the deeper truths about Bradman, the man and the cricketer, and the real nature of his contribution, not just to cricket but to Australia as a whole, finally became clear to me while researching this book.

True, he was endowed with superb physical abilities. But the real secret to his success was the fact he combined this agility and keenness of eye with a superior intelligence and a fierce, single-minded concentration that lifted his performances to near superhuman levels.

And he performed these feats against a background of personal turmoil: excruciating and debilitating illness, petty jealousies, carping criticisms and the ceaseless pressures caused by mass public adulation.

Behind Bradman the cricketer is a most extraordinary human being, a man of scrupulous honesty and depth of understanding. There are numerous rarely told stories about his kindness, like the night in London he was walking home from the theatre when he saw a group of derelicts huddled in the cold beside the River Thames. He bought them all food. When one asked him his name he simply pressed a crown into the man's hand and smiled as he walked away. His kindness to children and support for their charities is almost a legend in itself.

Despite his share of envious detractors, Bradman earned fierce loyalty on and off the field. Sam Loxton, a member of the 1948 side, paid this simple tribute: "The greatest privilege of my sporting life has been to be associated with Bradman."

Those who have only read about Bradman probably can't fully grasp the impact he had on cricket and society in his day. He was more than just a cricketer. During the 1930s in particular his flashing bat captured the hearts and minds of millions of people around the world and, in depression-torn Australia, lifted the spirits of a nation in a way that no politician or combination of events could manage.

Bradman's presence at the crease was always the cause of instant national attention. His great mate and often batting partner, Bill Brown, said that whenever Bradman came in to bat there was an overwhelming sense that something transcending the normal was about to happen, and usually did.

Now in his 86th year, Sir Donald still exudes greatness, even by his very presence. Yet, despite his Knighthood and all that world-wide fame has given him, he still prefers to think of himself simply as Don Bradman, the "boy from Bowral". Of similar homely philosophy is Lady Bradman, a person of immense charm who, deservedly, has shared in many of Sir Donald's triumphs and, during a long and happy marriage, has played her part in helping shape a great man's destiny

While I was researching this book, Sir Donald and Lady Bradman welcomed me into their home. The memory of that occasion will always be with me. They were the most gracious of hosts. I will always recall their hospitality with great kindness. I remain indebted to them for their assistance, particularly for allowing me to view their private photographs.

This book pays tribute to Sir Donald and his extraordinary talents. Equally, it honours two very fine people who have helped make the world a better place.

Peter Allen
Co-publisher

Bradman - The Man and the Legend

Don Bradman - 1932.

The eyes have it. Look at the baby Bradman. Look how the eyes shone with bold challenge, just 18 months after first opening on the world, when the legend was born. Look how sharp and clear they are, like transparent icicles [see photograph page 12].

The jaw and the mouth have it. Look at the determined way in which they are set. There is self-confidence here already. It's the optimism of the young, touched with an awareness that commonly awaits more mature years. It's as if this child of 18 months knows there are mountains to climb and that he will scale their dizzy heights.

The hands have it, too, at least the right one, which is easier to see in this old photograph. It has gripped the chair, much in the way it will later grip a cricket bat. This is the grip of someone who understands that the world must be grasped by action rather than contemplation, that the hand, as much as the eye, is at life's cutting edge.

And the feet, the dancing feet. It's remarkable how many people noticed how small they were. These are the feet whose prints mark the sands of time. They will never run out.

It is easy to see these qualities, of course, with hindsight. What did his parents, Emily and George Bradman, see when they presented their son to the photographer in a dress, after the fashion of 1910? They gave the boy their love and their solid common sense. They could not have seen what he would give his country and the sporting world. They could not have seen they had a legend on their hands.

The look changed little as the legend grew although, as the child became the youth and self-confidence blossomed, the slightly lopsided smile became more evident.

Neville Cardus wrote about the face in 1934, after youth had become man and climbed many of his mountains. Cardus was a critic and friend. At the end of the first day of the Leeds Test in 1934, the Australian team had lost three wickets for 39 runs in reply to England's 200, with Bradman to bat next day to save his country. Cardus invited Bradman to dinner. Bradman declined: "Thanks, but I've got to make 200 tomorrow at least." Cardus reminded Bradman that he had scored 334 at Leeds in 1930, so the law of averages was against his scoring 200 again. "I don't believe in the law of averages," said Bradman. He was 271 by Saturday night. He went on to 304.

Cardus wrote: "It is a jauntily confident face, isn't it? Eyes and mouth surely never conveyed a plainer message of abundant self-reliance. It is there...in the shrewd half-pucker of the eyes, with their air of watching your next move in the secure knowledge that you won't make anything of it at this individual's expense anyway. The little creases at the eyes lead directly somehow to the cocksure smile... Quite a pronounced smile it is, though the lips never forsake their curiously tight line...it seems to be the smile not so much of spontaneous amusement...as of a superiority that knows it can be discomfiting to the people who

measure themselves against it. It belongs to a man who knows not only exactly what he can do but also how few other people can do anything like it."

It is difficult to separate the man from the legend except, perhaps, to focus on the man as a matter of facts and to consider the legend as a spiritual side to the facts. Bradman was a legend in his own youthtime. The combination of man and legend has brought, at Bowral, the first museum ever devoted to an Australian in his or her lifetime.

Bradman said in 1938 that his ambition once was to be a house decorator. After his retirement, he nominated his 254 at Lords in 1930 as the most technically satisfying innings of his career because, with one or two exceptions, every ball went exactly where he intended it to go. "Any artist must surely aim at perfection," he said. The would-be decorator was prepared to admit to artistry, without being betrayed by artistic temperament. This is part of the legend.

The facts of the man go back to his parents, that photograph of the boy in the dress and to his first real match, aged 11, for his Bowral school team. He went to the crease to stop a hat-trick and scored 55 not out. His first century came next season. From then on he made a century about every third innings. Few people appreciate how the speed with which Bradman accumulated his runs complemented the security of his wicket. He hit 105 before lunch at Leeds and 309 in a day. He scored 200 runs or more in a single day 27 times in his first-class career. His 117 first-class hundreds took an average 128 minutes to reach.

Of all batsmen with more than 1000 Test runs, Sid Barnes comes second to Bradman's 99.94 average with 63.05. Brian Lara's average after 26 test innings was 62.62. No one sportsperson, according to the figures, has so dominated a sport. "He did not mean to be just one of the stars," wrote R.C. Robertson-Glasgow, "but the sun itself." Some spectators who saw his 100th century against the Indians in 1947 vowed never to go to the SCG again, content with incandescent memories.

In 1939 he had 21 lines in the English *Who's Who*, only eight fewer than Hitler, the man who started World War II, and 17 more than Stalin. The *New York Times*, serving a public that never sees cricket, saluted him in an editorial after he was knighted, describing Sir Donald as cricket's "unchallenged shining light".

To be a legend is a very public affair. To keep one's head at the same time is a challenge failed by many a hero and star. Bradman has succeeded off the field almost as brilliantly as he succeeded on it, as if he never inhaled the flattery. Tragedy is not in him because he hasn't devoted time to being famous. Despite the profligacy of his run-making, he carries in his soul, and in the brain behind that face, the solid qualities of the Australian bush and suburbs. As a cricketer he took the breath away. He remains an Australian *in excelsis*.

Tony Stephens

Don Bradman stands supreme as the most devastating run-maker in the history of cricket. When he retired in 1949 after gracing the world's cricket stage for more than two decades, England Captain, N.W.D. Yardley, said they were not only saying goodbye to the world's greatest cricketer, but also a great sportsman, on and off the field. Sir Donald Bradman has been called the greatest living Australian and a National Treasure. This photograph of him in 1949, walking out to bat at the Sydney Cricket Ground for the last time at the end of his marvellous career, evokes powerful memories. *Images of Bradman* will stir the memories of all who saw him play and bring to those who didn't some understanding why, nearly 46 years after his retirement, his legend lives on and why there will only ever be one Bradman.

"In the many pictures that I have stored in my mind from the 'burnt-out' Junes of forty years, there is none more dramatic or compelling than that of Bradman's small, serenely-moving figure in its big-peaked green cap coming out of the pavilion shadows into the sunshine, with the concentration, ardour and apprehension of surrounding thousands centred upon him and the destiny of a Test match in his hands."
　　　- English cricket historian,
　　　H.S. Altham, 1941.

Sir Donald Bradman described this sentence as the *"most moving about me"* he had ever read.

Donald George Bradman was born at Cootamundra, NSW, on August 27, 1908. His grandfather, Charles Bradman, had migrated from Suffolk, England, aged 19, in 1852 and settled in the Southern Highlands of NSW where he met and married

Elizabeth Biffen of Mittagong, a small township near Bowral. Soon after, they moved west to a farm at Jindalee in the Cootamundra district. They raised a family of six children, including Don Bradman's father, George, who also married a Mittagong girl, Emily Whatman, in

1893. Like his father, he took up land in the Cootamundra district, at Yeo Yeo. George and Emily had five children. Don Bradman was the youngest. In 1911, George Bradman decided to move his family to Bowral, where a cricket legend began.

Right: One of the earliest surviving photographs of Donald Bradman, aged about 18 months, when his parents, Emily and George Bradman, still lived at Yeo Yeo, near Cootamundra, NSW. The family moved to Bowral, in the Southern Highlands of NSW, about a year after this photograph was taken.

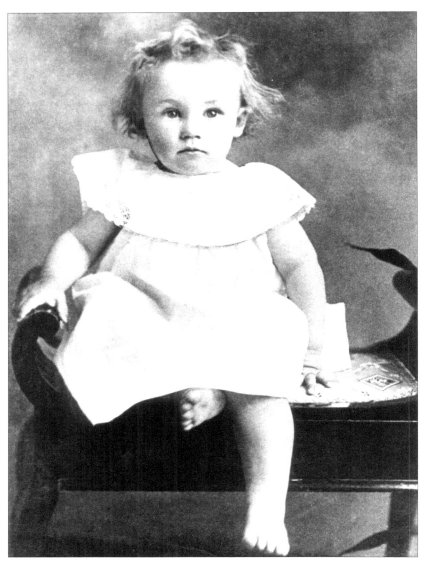

Above: Sir Donald Bradman's immediate ancestors, his grandfather and grandmother, Charles and Elizabeth Bradman, and his father, George, aged about 12. From Sir Donald's private collection, the photograph was taken when the family lived near Cootamundra. Charles and Elizabeth Bradman are buried in the Cootamundra cemetery.

Above: The house at Cootamundra, NSW, where he was born.

Above: The slab hut at Yeo Yeo where he lived until he was nearly three.

Above: Aged about three, outside his parents', home in Shepherd Street, Bowral.

This house in Shepherd Street, Bowral, forms an historic part of the Bradman legend. Behind it, Bradman as a boy practised his cricket skills against a round brick tankstand using a stump and golf ball and, mainly for amusement, devised his own game of Test cricket, playing the roles of famous batsmen of the day. In his book, *Farewell to Cricket*, published in 1950, Sir Donald wrote :

Many times I incurred mother's displeasure because I had to finish some important Test Match at the very moment she wanted me for a meal... Looking back over the years, I can understand how it must have developed the co-ordination of brain, eye and muscle which was to serve me so well in important matches later on.

During his early boyhood practice sessions he often cajoled both his mother and father to bowl to him. In 1924 the family moved to a new house his father built, in Glebe Street, Bowral, and still standing opposite what is now Bradman Oval, the site of The Bradman Museum.

Above: A young Don Bradman, in his Bowral School uniform with the family dog, Teddy.

Left: Taking block, at the age of 12, when he scored his first century, 115 not out, playing for Bowral School against Mittagong School.

He recalls his pride was short lived.

Next day we were lined up in the playground and the headmaster said: 'I understand that there is a certain boy among you who scored a century yesterday against Mittagong. Well, that is no reason or excuse why you should have left a bat behind.' I was never guilty of the same offence again.
        - Farewell to Cricket, 1950.

13

Above: Youngest sister, May, photographed at Bowral. Apart from Sir Donald, she is the only survivor of the five Bradman children.

Above: Don Bradman's parents, George and Emily Bradman, photographed at Bowral in the 1930s.

Above: Sister Lilian, seen during the early Bowral days. She taught him to play the piano, and helped instil in him a great love of music.

Left: This was proudly known in the Bradman family as "father's fence". George Bradman, a highly skilled carpenter, built the arrow-straight, ornate post and rail fence along the border of a Bowral property. Sir Donald recalls his father constructed it single-handed, using crowbar and shovel to dig the holes.

My parents taught me to be a cricketer off the field as well as on. It was not 'did you win', but 'did you play the game?' that made the man.
    - Don Bradman speaking at a public farewell in Bowral before the 1930 England Tour.

Aged eight years, with his brother, Victor, who, later, also played cricket for Bowral, but readily confessed he didn't possess any of his brother Don's cricketing abilities. Vic Bradman lived his life in relative obscurity as owner of a menswear store in Bowral. He died at the age of 55.

Above: Jessie Menzies, who became Mrs Don Bradman in 1932, went to the same Bowral school as Don Bradman. The daughter of a local farmer, she is seen here [second from the left] with three school-mates. The Bradman and Menzies families were close friends. Jessie boarded with the Bradmans during her first year at school.

Above: Vic [left] and Don Bradman in their Sunday best in the backyard of their Glebe Street, Bowral, home. It was taken at or about the same time as the photograph on the left.

At the end of 1922 Bradman left school and took a position as a clerk in a Bowral real estate agency, owned by Mr Percy Westbrook. He was still a Westbrook employee when this photograph was taken about 1924. Percy Westbrook played a crucial role in his early career by giving him the time to play cricket in Sydney when the offer came in 1926. Bradman paid this tribute to him at a farewell function in Bowral on the eve of the 1930 England tour:

•After leaving school I spent five years with Mr Westbrook before going to Sydney. Everything lay in his hands, but at great inconvenience he let me go to Sydney. It was due to him that I got my chance in big cricket.•

This historic photograph from Sir Donald's private collection shows the Bowral Town cricket team during the playing days of his father, George, who is in the back row fourth from the right. Bradman and his father never played together, although he later played with a number of the men in the photograph. One of them, his uncle, Dick Whatman, is kneeling in the centre of the picture.

A 1927 club cricket match in progress at Glebe Park, Bowral, where Don Bradman first came to notice as a batsman. He played in the match, but isn't in the photograph, although his father, George, is one of the umpires..

Also from Sir Donald's private collection, this photograph shows Alf Stephens taking block in his backyard nets where Bradman, as a teenager, often practised. A Bowral builder and keen local cricketer, Alf Stephens employed George Bradman as a carpenter after the family moved from Cootamundra and did much to foster young Don Bradman's cricketing talents. He became a close personal friend and in 1930 travelled to England to watch Don play on his first overseas tour. Sir Donald wrote:

Mr Alf Stephens took a great interest in my career and journeyed to England more than once to watch the Test Matches on the other side of the world.

Below Left: Alf Stephens

Below Right: Stephens' cricket pitch in the grounds of his home in Aitken Road, Bowral.

Alf Stephens outside the Bradman home George Bradman built in Glebe Street, Bowral, in 1924. The Bradman Foundation now owns the house.

Players and officials from the Bowral and Mittagong teams, taken at Glebe Park, Bowral, in 1925. Don Bradman is in the second row wearing a cap. His father, George Bradman, is in the back row [far right] wearing a hat. His uncle and Captain of the Bowral team, Dick Whatman, is in the middle row with the cap and grey moustache. Bradman had actually made his first appearance with the Bowral side four years earlier, aged 13, when, as the team's scorer, he was called on to bat after a player failed to show up. Using a man's full-sized bat, almost as tall as he was, he scored 29 not out, but, as he wrote later, he didn't become a regular member of the side until 1925:

With the beginning of the summer of 1925, I really commenced my serious cricket career as a regular member of the Bowral Team. I was only seventeen. Some of my colleagues were in the forties. I deemed it quite a privilege to have the opportunity of playing with these grown-up men.
- Farewell to Cricket, 1950.

Photographed in 1926, aged 17, towards the end of his first season [1925-1926] as a regular member of the Bowral Town cricket team. By a co-incidence of history it was during this season he first faced a demon bowler named Bill O'Reilly, from neighbouring Wingello, and set a Berrima District record with a score of 234 in their very first encounter. Bradman scored the runs on the first afternoon of the match, thrashing the ball to all parts of the ground, an "unmerciful belting" as O'Reilly later ruefully observed. The boy Bradman was not out at the end of the day's play. O'Reilly, however, had his revenge when play resumed the following weekend. He bowled Bradman first ball. When their careers ended more than 20 years later they were described as the "world's greatest batsman" and the "world's greatest bowler". Later that year Bradman broke his own district record with a score of 300 and finished the 1925-1926 season with 1,318 runs at an average of 94.14. He took 51 wickets at an average of 7.8 and held 26 catches. His fame for prodigious scoring spread beyond Bowral and led to his first invitation from the NSW Cricket Association to attend a practice session before the State selectors at the Sydney Cricket Ground. A sports writer wrote that Bradman turned up wearing black braces. Bradman said:

It might make a good story but it wasn't true.

Below: Jessie Menzies about the time Bradman first played grade cricket in Sydney.

The Bradman grip.

Bradman's impressive SCG trial resulted in an invitation to play grade cricket in Sydney, ultimately with St. George, and his selection in a one-day State trial at the SCG No 1, thereby realising a boyhood dream. After watching Australia play England in a Test Match there in 1921 he said to his father: "*I shall never be satisfied until I play on this ground.*" The nets trial drew attention to another aspect of Bradman's play, his unorthodox batting grip, the subject of considerable discussion. It differed from other players because his left hand was turned over so far the wrist was at the back of the handle of the bat. A number of senior players advised him to change, but, as he explained in *Farewell to Cricket*, he decided against it:

My grip, developed on concrete wickets, was different from that of most players. It assisted me in pulling the ball and was much safer for on-side shots, though it handicapped me somewhat in playing the ball between mid-off and point. I experimented and worked out the pros and cons and eventually decided not to change my natural grip. Throughout a long career my grip caused many arguments, but I think it is sufficient to prove that any young player should be allowed to develop his own natural style providing he is not revealing any obvious error. A player is not necessarily wrong because he is different.

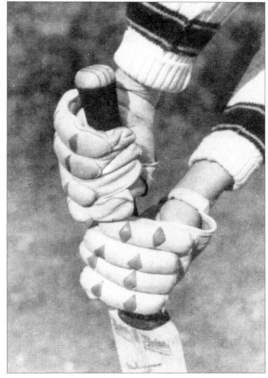

The grip and easy stance.

Demonstrating a back defensive stroke.

Note the turned left hand.

The 1926 Southern Country Week team.

Back Row – A. Sieler, M. Linder, E. Chapman, A. Brice, K. Murray, H. McGuick, G. Coulter.
Front Row – N. Broderick, H. Webster, L. Sieler (Captain), J. Gray, D.G. Bradman.

Soon after the SCG trial a boyish Bradman, seated on the far right, won a place in the 1926 Southern Country Week team after scoring 62 not out [retired] and taking four wickets for 35 in an inter-district match for Southern Districts against the South Coast. His Country Week performances in November, 1926, led to his selection for Combined Country against Combined City. In that match he further pressed his claim for State selection with a score of 98, and, as he later recorded, played for the first time against the great Test batsman, Charles Macartney:

It was a great thrill to play for the first time against such a brilliant batsman as Charlie Macartney. Although I had to chase a number of his shots I delighted in seeing him score 126 against us.

Bowral railway station holds particular memories for Sir Donald. In his early days of playing grade cricket for the St. George Club he used to catch the train from there to Sydney every Saturday morning, rising before 5 am and not getting home until midnight.

1927 - 1928

While his formative years, both on and off the cricket field, are an essential part of the Bradman legend, it had its real beginnings in the 1927-1928 season with the start of his first-class cricket career. The boy from Bowral, as he'd become known, immediately captured attention with a dashing 118 in his first-class debut for NSW against South Australia, an innings that bordered on the precocious when the 19-year-old hit Australia's best spin bowler, Clarrie Grimmett, for two fours in his first over. No one realised it then, but such aggression was to become his trademark and help him hold sway over world cricket for much of the next two decades. Later that season he scored another century, 134 not out against Victoria, and finished the season with a Sheffield Shield aggregate of 416 and an average of 46.22. Don Bradman, the cricketing genius, had arrived.

Despite top-scoring with 43 for a NSW Second XI v Victoria at the SCG in January, 1927, he had to wait until the start of the 1927-1928 season to win his first NSW Sheffield Shield cap and blazer. He is shown here proudly wearing his second XI cap and blazer for a family photograph, taken in the backyard of his Glebe Street, Bowral, home. Bradman played his first match for NSW against Broken Hill en route to Adelaide for the Sheffield Shield match against South Australia in December, 1927. He scored 46 in Broken Hill and then went on to score a brilliant century [118] in his first-class debut in Adelaide.

"Though only 19 years old he played like a veteran, devoid of nerves, cracking Grimmett twice for four at the very outset of his innings and completing his hundred by sweeping Lee to the leg boundary."
    - A Press report on Bradman's maiden first-class century.

The NSW Sheffield Shield team, December, 1927.

Back Row – N. Phillips, F. Jordan, A. Scanes, S. Everett, T.J. Andrews, D.G. Bradman,
A. Jackson, W.A. Oldfield.
Front Row – G. Morgan, A.F. Kippax [Captain], Dr F.V. McAdam [Manager],
R. McNamee, A. Mailey.

This was Bradman's first tour for NSW. The team played matches against South Australia and Victoria. In the first match against South Australia Bradman was to have been 12th man but played when Archie Jackson couldn't take the field because of a boil on the knee, which had also kept him out of the Broken Hill game. Bradman's innings of 118 was widely hailed. NSW lost the match despite batting first and scoring 519 in the first innings. Apart from the cricket, he relished his first meeting with the great slow leg-break bowler, Clarrie Grimmett:

I treasured the opportunity to meet Clarrie Grimmett and watching the way he could spin a soft rubber ball on a table. I have never seen anybody who can make the ball perform such tricks. At the time, I thought Grimmett was the best slow leg-break bowler I had played against. With the passing of time I see no reason to change my opinion.
- Farewell to Cricket, 1950.

Clarrie Grimmett.

Charles Bannerman, the first man to score a century in Test cricket, 165 not out for Australia against England in 1876-1877, appears to be giving the young Don Bradman some fatherly encouragement in this photograph taken during the 1927-1928 season.

Arthur Mailey's *Bohemians* at Dudauman, NSW, in 1928.

Ginger Meggs meets Bradman. From the original Bancks cartoon, drawn in 1931.

Shown here wearing their specially tailored striped blazers, the *Bohemians* played a number of second-class matches in NSW country centres, including Bradman's birthplace, Cootamundra, where he was dismissed for only one. Bradman is squatting in the front row, third from the left, alongside his captain, Arthur Mailey. Standing fourth from the right in cap and jumper is J.C. Bancks, creator of the comic strip, *Ginger Meggs*.

It was disappointing for me to be run out for one the only time I played in my birthplace.
- *Farewell to Cricket, 1950.*

Bradman by Arthur Mailey.

With England due on tour, the young Bowral batsman had become one of the most talked-about cricketers in Australia at the start of the 1928-1929 season. He confirmed his exciting early promise with a century in each innings for NSW v Queensland, ensuring his selection in the Australian side for the First Test. He failed to hold his place in the Second Test, but was chosen for the Third, and was never again dropped from an Australian team. He averaged 66.85 in the Tests and 148.83 in Sheffield Shield matches during this season. The young Don Bradman had become a household name when the legendary Australian poet and author A.B. "Banjo" Paterson observed him in a Sydney sports store, and asked of a knowledge-able salesman behind the counter: "Is he going to be as good as Trumper?" Years later, Paterson recalled the meeting and the salesman's astute reply about Bradman's cricket potential. Paterson's reminiscence appears below.

A couple of years ago I was in a sports depot in Sydney and a wiry sunburnt young bush chap came in, and started looking over the goods. I've had so much to do with athletes I can generally pick a man fairly well, and I said to the salesman, 'That's a hard-looking young fellow and he's very light on his feet. I should say he had done some boxing or was accustomed to riding rough horses. They have to be pretty active for that game.'

So the salesman laughed and said, 'No, you're a bit out. But he's a somebody all the same.' I said, "Who is he?"

'Oh,' he said, 'that's Don Bradman, this new boy wonder crick-eter they have just discovered.'

You see he was only Don Bradman, the Bowral boy then, and hadn't been to England. He's Mr Bradman now, and many congratulations to him.

So the salesman brought the boy over - he seemed only a boy to me - and after we had exchanged a few remarks, Bradman went out. So then I asked the inevitable questions: I said, 'How good is this fellow? Is he going to be as good as Trumper?'

Now, the salesman had been a first-class cricketer himself and he gave me what I consider a very clear summing-up of the two men.

A SOMEBODY
by A. B. "Banjo" Paterson

'Well,' he said, 'when Trumper got onto good wickets he developed a beautiful free style, like a golfer that plays a full swing with a good follow-through. He trusted the ball to come true off the wicket, and if it bumped, or shot, or kicked, he might be apt to get out. But this Bradman takes nothing to trust. Even after he has got onto good wickets, he won't trust the ball a foot, and he watches every ball till the last moment before he hits it. His eye is so good and his movements are so quick that he can hit the ball to the fence without any swing at all. That makes him look a bit rough in style compared with Trumper, and he hits across his wicket a lot. They say that's a fatal thing to do, but I never saw him miss one of them.'

So I said, 'You wouldn't remember W.G. Grace, can you remember Ranjitsinhji?'

'Yes,' he said, 'Ranji had a beautiful style, but he was a bit fond of playing to the gallery. If he'd like to stonewall, they'd never have got him out, but he used to do exhibition shots - late cuts, and tricky little leg glances - and out he'd go. There's no exhibition shots about this Bradman.'

I said, 'How will he get on in England? Will he handle the English wickets?'

'Yes,' he said, 'don't worry about him on English wickets. He'd play on a treacle wicket or on a corrugated iron wicket. He's used to kerosene tin wickets up there in Bowral. He'll never be the world's most artistic cricketer, but he'll be the world's hardest wicket to get out.'

Well, it's not often that a prediction works out as well as that, it is?

From a radio talk reproduced in Song Of The Pen: A.B. 'Banjo' Paterson Complete Works, 1901-1941.

Don Bradman's path to international fame began when selected to play for NSW against the visiting MCC side in Sydney in November, 1928, his first encounter against such English greats as Tate, Larwood and Walter Hammond, who later wrote he remembered Bradman as a "*slim, shortish boy with a grim nervous face. He looked about 19 and not very formidable*". Hammond quickly realised the error of his judgment when Bradman first ran him out with a lightning return and then went on to dominate the MCC bowling with scores of 87 and 132 not out.

His efforts against the MCC and centuries in each innings in the NSW v Queensland Sheffield Shield match a few days before, helped win Bradman his first Test cap, against England in the First Test in Brisbane, in November-December, 1928. Below he is seen proudly wearing his first Australian XI blazer. He was aged 20. Bradman heard of his selection under unusual circumstances:

On the night in question, the names of the chosen were to be broadcast. There was some delay, so I retired to bed, but had not gone to sleep when a nearby wireless gave out the names. They were in alphabetical order and therefore mine was first on the list. So this ambition had been achieved.
- *Farewell to Cricket, 1950.*

Above: Practising in the nets in Brisbane before the NSW v Queensland Shield match in 1928. He scored a century in each innings.

Above: Wearing his first Test blazer and cap.

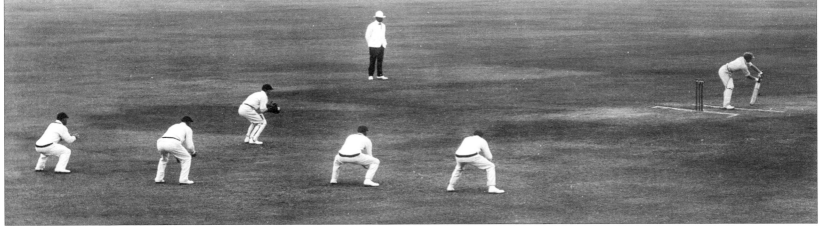

Below: Bradman strikes an odd pose defending against Larwood in a match for NSW against England at the SCG in 1928-1929.

A rare shot of Bradman playing in his first Test match, versus England in Brisbane, December, 1928. He scored 18 and one.

Bradman's 18 and one reflected his team's ill fortunes in the First Test. It was an unhappy match for Australia. England inflicted the heaviest defeat ever on an Australian XI, winning by the huge margin of 675 runs. Chasing England's 521 in the first innings and 342 for 8 declared in the second, Australia replied with only 122 in the first and 66 in the second when caught on a wet wicket. Bradman, out second ball, had never batted on a wet wicket before.

What a thrashing we got. For me it was a real grounding... I did not even mind being dismissed for 18 runs in our first innings, for my form had been quite good up to the time Maurice Tate defeated me with a slower ball. But it was a great disappointment to bat on a sticky wicket in our second innings [the first time I had ever seen one] and find I knew absolutely nothing about that kind of wicket.
  - Farewell to Cricket, 1950.

Out lbw to Tate for 18, in a short, impressive first innings.

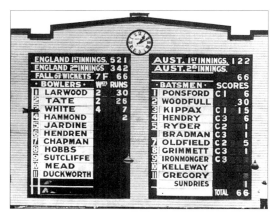

The First Test scoreboard showing Australia all out for 66, Bradman, one.

The Australian team v England, Second Test, Sydney, December, 1928.

Back Row – W.M. Woodfull, W.H. Ponsford, H. Ironmonger, D.J. Blackie, O.E. Nothling, H.L. Hendry.
Front Row – V.Y. Richardson, C.V. Grimmett, J.S. Ryder [Captain], D.G. Bradman [12th man], W.A. Oldfield, A.F. Kippax.

Despite a public clamour for him not be "dropped like a hot coal" after his first experience in Test cricket, Bradman was relegated to twelfth man, although he ended up fielding through the entire England first innings after Bill Ponsford suffered a broken bone in the hand batting against Larwood. Australia were again soundly beaten.

Bradman regained his place in the Australian side for the Third Test against England in Melbourne in January, 1929. He redeemed himself by scoring 79 in the first innings, then in the second innings made his first Test century, 112, in only his second Test match. Up till that time, he was the youngest player, 20 years 129 days, ever to score a Test century. Australia lost the Test, but this time by only three wickets. After watching Bradman's century, Charles Macartney wrote :

"Bradman is a wonderful find for Australia... Although his chief asset at present is confidence and pluck, he has made a remarkable improvement in his actual play during his very short career in first-class cricket. He is going to be one of the finest players Australia has produced."

Apart from his own century, Bradman well remembered the Test for the England batsmen's mastery on a sticky wicket, especially Herbert Sutcliffe, who scored 135.

•Hobbs and Sutcliffe were caught on a really bad one... Even now I think Sutcliffe's exhibition that day was the nearest approach to mastery on a sticky wicket I saw throughout my career... His uncanny ability to let the ball go when it jumped or turned was simply amazing.•

    - Farewell to Cricket, 1950.

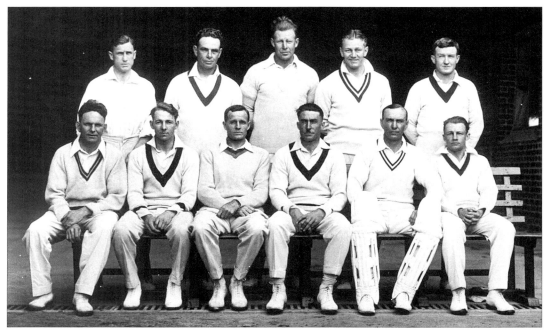

In the lead-up to the Tests, Bradman, seated far right, played for The Rest v Australia. Vic Richardson captained The Rest and Bill Woodfull, Australia.

Stretching to reach his ground in the Third Test v England, 1929, although the wicket-keeper doesn't look too interested.

Herbert Sutcliffe in the nets.

Sutcliffe, always impeccable.

Bradman and Jackson.

Archie Jackson, the batting genius
who died tragically at the age of only 23.

Following the Third Test, the
Australian selectors cast around for
a new Fourth Test opening partner for
Bill Ponsford. Vic Richardson had failed
with only 35 in four innings. Bradman
was tried as an experimental opener for
NSW against South Australia, but Tim
Wall dismissed him for five in the first
innings and two in the second.
Richardson's place in the Fourth Test
went to the richly endowed Archie
Jackson, who had scored 162 and 90
against South Australia. Bradman and

Jackson [seen here together] became
firm friends, first as NSW, then
Australian team mates and were to figure in many historic batting partnerships. Tragically, Jackson died from
tuberculosis in 1933, at the age of only
23. Bradman was a pallbearer at his
funeral. In the Fourth Test Australia lost
by only 12 runs. Jackson displayed all
his extravagant talents with a masterful
164, an innings still regarded as one of
the finest in the history of the game. In
Farewell to Cricket, Sir Donald, who

batted with him, makes special mention
of Jackson's century that day:

*What an innings he played! Jackson,
who was then 19, opened the batting
and in half an hour saw Woodfull,
Hendry and Kippax back in the pavilion with the total at 19. Undaunted by
this setback, Jackson proceeded to play
an innings which from the point of view
of stroke execution, elegance and sheer
artistry held the spectators as few
innings in history have done.*

With his keen eyesight, lightning reflexes and marvellous ball sense, it was no surprise that Bradman became a superb tennis player. But for his decision to concentrate on cricket, it is almost certain he would have played tennis at the very highest international level. This snapshot, taken in Adelaide in 1929, shows him during a match with Jean Wilson and R.V. Thomas, a former Wimbledon doubles champion.

In January 1929, on the eve of the NSW v Victoria Sheffield Shield match, Bradman agreed to have his name on a bat manufactured by the English firm William Sykes Ltd. To mark the occasion, the company gave him a new, unoiled, unprepared bat to use in the match. In a virtuoso performance, in which he broke record after record, Bradman responded by scoring 340 not out, then the highest score ever made on the Sydney Cricket Ground. The bat, photographed here, was returned to England for display and never used again.

Wearing the special cap presented to him by J.J. Giltinan to commemorate his record 340 not out against Victoria. Mr Giltinan and Test cricketer, Victor Trumper, played a major role in establishing Rugby League in NSW.

Don Bradman, Alan Fairfax and Archie Jackson.

The selectors' policy of introducing younger players to Test cricket paid off in the Fifth Test against England, at the Melbourne Cricket Ground in March, 1929, when Australia scored a memorable five-wicket victory. The three NSW youngsters photographed here, Bradman, Fairfax and Jackson, played significant roles in Australia's resurgence. As well as scoring 123 and 37 not out, Bradman figured in a dramatic, record-breaking fifth-wicket partnership of 183 with Alan Fairfax. When Bradman reached his century the ecstasy of the crowd reached such heights that a journalist later wrote: "Such hero-worship comes to few men in their time." In his 1983 *Bradman* biography, author, Michael Page, observed this phrase might well stand as *"an epigraph on the great monolith of Don Bradman's career"*. Bradman ended the 1928-1929 season with many records to his name, including having scored more runs [468] in a Test series before he was 21 than any other cricketer. His first-class aggregate for the season was 1,690 runs, also a record.

As in all seasons leading up to an England Tour, the 1929-1930 Australian season was of particular importance to players vying for Test spots. Don Bradman ensured his place on the boat to England with devastating certainty. He opened his first-class performances with 157 against a visiting MCC side, followed this with a century and double century, in one day, playing in a Woodfull XI v J. Ryder XI trial match in Sydney and then, mixed in with a string of other Sheffield Shield successes, scored 452 not out against Queensland to set a new world record for the highest score in first-class cricket. His Shield aggregate for the season, 894, broke the record he set in 1928-1929 by one run. His first-class average in all matches, 113.28, set another record, then the highest ever by a NSW batsman. *The Bradman Albums* recall his pride on his selection for his first England tour. He wrote:

•*Selection for England, which is the goal of every Australian cricketer, made me feel proud that I had lived up to the hopes and ambitions of my parents and friends.*•

Left: Bradman was much in demand in 1929-1930 playing in second-class promotional matches. These included 13 games in NSW country towns, among them Moree, where he posed with this horse named Charger during a visit to the Leadingham property. He scored 13 not out and 96 in the Moree match.

Right: Another country tour in 1929-1930 was with a Bill Tidmarsh XI to Narooma and Bega on the NSW South Coast. Seen here outside a Narooma hotel where the team stayed, Bradman scored 107 not out against Narooma and 127 not out against Bega.

A photograph from Sir Donald's personal collection. It was taken in 1930.

Driving Clarrie Grimmett in the W. Woodfull XI v J. Ryder XI trial at the Sydney Cricket Ground in December, 1929.

He achieved a unique and unusual double in the Woodfull-Ryder trial match. Ryder's team, which ultimately won in an exciting finish by only one wicket, batted first and scored 663. Woodfull's side was forced to follow on, after scoring only 309, with Bradman last man out on 124. Woodfull sent Bradman back in to open the second innings. Before Grimmett finally bowled him, Bradman made 225, to record the remarkable achievement of completing a century and double century in the one day.

Bill Woodfull.

Returning to the SCG pavilion following his double century in
the Woodfull XI v Ryder XI trial..

Taking off for a run after cutting Hurwood during his world record breaking innings.

Bradman reached the scoring pinnacle of his career in a Sheffield Shield match between NSW and Queensland at the SCG in January, 1930, by breaking the world record for the highest score in first-class cricket. His 452 not out broke Bill Ponsford's previous record of 437. He had never before considered seeking records, but on this occasion decided to attempt it after being 205 not out on the first day of his innings, a Saturday. Play didn't resume until the Monday, enabling him to return to the crease rested and fresh. One of the first congratulatory telegrams was from an admiring and gracious Bill Ponsford. Bradman's 452 took 415 minutes. Ponsford's 437 took 621 minutes.

The SCG scoreboard showing his record 452.

A photo taken during Bradman's world record innings of 452 not out. It appears in his book *Farewell to Cricket*. The caption reads: "The author's idea of the proper way to follow through after making a full-blooded drive."

A famous posed shot of Bradman.

In *Farewell to Cricket*, he wrote of his record innings:

It was one of those occasions when everything went right. The wicket was true and firm, the outfield in good condition and the weather warm but not unduly hot... Upon reflection, it seemed incredible that in such a short space of time I should have achieved something which was beyond my wildest dreams when I first walked onto that beautiful Sydney ground. It was quite true that my batting still did not measure up to the canons of orthodoxy demanded by those who give style number one priority in the list of essentials of the batting art. This realisation did not worry me because I took the view that my style had been moulded under hard wicket conditions and could only be gradually modified as my experience on turf wickets was extended.

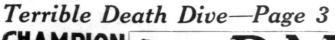

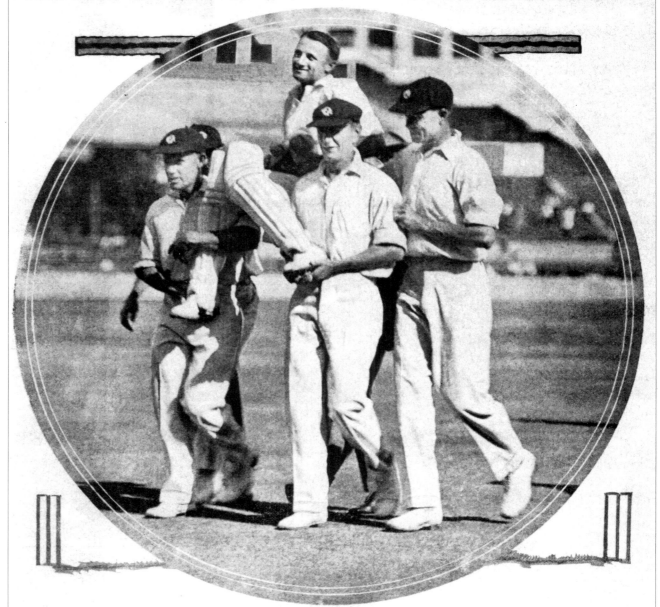

This is how Sydney's *Daily Telegraph Pictorial* acclaimed Bradman's world record breaking feat.
The photograph shows the Queensland players carrying him off the field.

Demonstrating his defensive technique during a special appearance at a Sydney store,
which was selling the William Sykes brand Bradman bat, the type he used in making his record score.

Left: Soon after the above photograph
was taken, Bradman was selected for his
first tour of England. Here he is seen
packing his suitcase, apparently with
some difficulty.

1930 England Tour

And so to England, where Don Bradman arrived with the words of Maurice Tate, during the Englishmen's 1927-1928 Australian Tour, still ringing in his ears. Tate had said: *"We shall see you in England. But keep your bat straighter, my boy. Those cross-bat shots will come to grief on our wickets."* Bradman conceded there was risk in some of his shots, particularly the leg-side pull shot, one of his favourites. But, undeterred by Tate's warning, he went to England determined to carry out his own theory that cricket was a test between bat and ball, and, despite the risks, was determined to continue playing attacking cricket *"unless the situation of the game or the tactics of the opposition made it impossible".* That decision was to prove devastating for England. The great English cricket writer Neville Cardus described part of Bradman's innings of 254 in the Lord's Test as *"a massacre, nothing less".* And Bradman sustained the *"massacre"* for much of the tour, amassing 3,170 runs in all matches. In the Tests, he scored 974, at an average of 139.14. In many ways the 1930 tour was the real launching platform for cricket's most remarkable career. And through it all, he never forgot Bowral. At a Bowral farewell before leaving he said:

• *This is the proudest evening of my life to be able to return to Bowral to say good-bye to the friends I made when a boy and to see those who helped me a bit along the road.•*

The Australian 1930 team for England.

Back Row – W.L.Kelly [Manager], A. Jackson, T. Wall, E.L. a'Beckett, P.M. Hornibrook,
A. Hurwood, C.V. Grimmett, T.H. Howard [Treasurer].
Sitting – A.G. Fairfax, W.H. Ponsford, V.Y. Richardson, W.M. Woodfull [Captain],
A.F. Kippax, D.G. Bradman, C.W. Walker.
Front Row – S.J. McCabe, W.A. Oldfield.

A marvellous action shot of Bradman practising in the nets in Perth during the 1930 team's stopover on the way to England. Bradman scored 27 in the Australian XI match against Western Australia. The team travelled to England on the RMS *Orford*.

Few people, not even his most ardent admirers, realised the devastating and demoralising effect that Bradman, not yet 22, would have on the English bowlers in 1930. In the following months the cover drive, demonstrated here, was repeated with aggressive regularity on grounds all around England.

Bradman gave the Englishmen an ominous sign of things to come when he scored 236 in 276 minutes in the opening match of the tour against Worcestershire in May, 1930, and 185 not out in the second match against Leicestershire. Here, he punishes a loose ball from Leicestershire bowler, Astill. His 236 against Worcestershire was the most successful debut on English wickets by any Australian batsman in cricket history.

Bradman and Woodfull going out to bat at Worcester.

Astill again on the receiving end of Bradman's bat in the match against Leicestershire.

In the office of L.A.W. Pearce. Shown here [left to right] are: Mrs Bert Oldfield, Betty Howard seated on the arm of Mrs Tom Howard's chair, Mrs F.M. Cush, Mrs R.L. Jones, Mrs Alan Kippax [seated], Mrs L.A.W. Pearce, F.M. Cush almost obscured by Mrs M. Oldfield, Miss May Bradman, Mrs George Bradman [seated], M.A. Noble, Archie Jackson's mother, E.A. Dwyer [partly obscured], Alan Fairfax's mother, George Bradman and R.L. Jones. L.A.W. Pearce is seated far right.

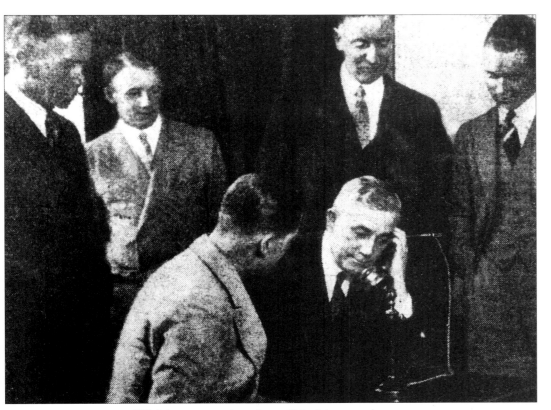

Waiting to receive the call in Liverpool were:
Left to right, standing – Arthur Mailey, Bradman, W.L. Kelly [team Manager] and Charlie Walker.
Seated – A.F. Kippax and T. Howard [talking on the phone].

The 1930 Australian cricketers became part of communications history on Monday, May 26, when they spoke to relatives and friends back in Australia on the newly established radio-telephone link between Australia and England. The line had only been open three weeks. Previous touring parties had to rely on letters and cablegrams for communication. The Australians were in Liverpool when the call came through in the early hours of the morning. Bradman spoke to several people including his mother and father and sister, May, later describing it as "*an uncanny feeling*". The relatives and friends made the call from the Sydney office of L.A.W. Pearce.

Delicately cutting past slips against Surrey.

In the County matches leading up to the Tests, Bradman continued to gain valuable experience under English conditions, and startled the English bowlers in the process. Against Surrey, he added to his list of double centuries with 252 not out. After the hard wickets and warm weather of Australia, he found English conditions difficult and unpleasant. He wrote:

•I found it difficult, for instance, to adjust myself to the idea of wearing sweater, blazer and overcoat before a roaring fire waiting my turn to bat.•
- Farewell To Cricket, 1950.

Going out to bat against Hampshire.

In the Hampshire match, he became the first touring batsman ever to score 1,000 runs before the end of May - the opening four weeks of the English season. To give him the chance to complete the feat, Woodfull sent Bradman in to open the Australian innings at 3.30 pm on May 31 in rainy conditions with fading light. Bradman needed 46 runs to reach his target. He made it with one run to spare, scoring 47 for a total of 1,001 runs, after hitting two fours off the last two balls before rain stopped play for the day. Bradman, who went on to score 191 when played resumed the next day, paid a gracious tribute to Hampshire's Captain, Lord Tennyson's sportsmanship. He wrote:

I feel there was a measure of generosity on the part of the Hampshire Captain in allowing play to continue when the weather might reasonably have caused a cessation. I was not unmindful of this when it fell to my lot in 1938 to close the Australian innings at Lord's and thereby give Bill Edrich the chance to score 1,000 runs in May.

Edrich also succeeded [see page 176].

Glancing Tyldesley in the First Test at Nottingham, June, 1930. Hammond is the fielder [right].
Batting on a rain-sodden pitch, Bradman made eight in the first innings and 131 in the second.

Australia lost the First Test by 93 runs. Bradman said of the defeat:

We were disillusioned but not disgraced. England gained victory by 93 runs, but Australia made 335 in the fourth innings, the highest total of the match. I contributed 131 of these, at one stage thought we might save the match, but Robins, the mercurial Middlesex spinner, bowled me with a 'wrong-un' at which I attempted no stroke.

Right: Bowled Robins for 131 in the second innings of the Nottingham Test.

Bradman's great appreciation of music ensured that one of his most memorable nights on the 1930 tour was when the Australian cricketers were special guests at the Royal Albert Hall, London, for a performance of the musical, *Hiawatha*. He is seen here shaking hands with the famous Australian singer, Harold Williams, who played the lead role.

Above: Like whole generations of top-line cricketers, Bradman enjoyed playing golf to relax from the rigours of cricket. Here, he is hitting off in a rain-plagued round at the West Kent Course in June, 1930. The other players are J.C. Bancks, creator of *Ginger Meggs* [second from left], Arthur Mailey, partly obscured by Bradman, and Alan Kippax under the umbrella behind Bradman.

Right: Bradman and Kippax shelter under umbrellas during the round.

Playing to Gubby Allen at silly leg in the Second Test at Lord's.

Acknowledging the cheers of the Lord's crowd after completing his 200.

The Second Test of the 1930 tour, played at Lord's, sent pulses racing among all who watched and became, as Sir Donald Bradman wrote in 1950, *"one of those glorious chapters in cricket which connoisseurs revel in discussing by the fireside"*. Bradman, seen above playing a ball from Tate to Allen at silly leg, scored 254 in the first innings, which he himself considers to be the most technically perfect he ever played [see page 55]. The one indifferent shot was the one that got him out. Neville Cardus, whose description of Bradman's innings appears on the next page, called it a game that *"could be laid up in heaven"* and the *"greatest Test match I ever saw"*. Australia eventually won a game of dramatic twists and turns by seven wickets to level the series at 1-all.

Gubby Allen.

THE IDEAL CRICKET MATCH

[An extract]

By Sir Neville Cardus

If some good fairy were to ask me to pick one match of all I have seen, to relive it as I lived it at the time when it happened, my choice would be easy: England v Australia at Lord's in June, 1930. This game could be laid up in heaven, a Platonic idea of cricket in perfection. It was limited to four days and finished at five o'clock on the closing afternoon; 1,601 runs were scored and 29 wickets fell. Bradman batted in a Test at Lord's for the first time, scoring 254 in his first innings. England batted first and made 425, but lost by seven wickets. Glorious sunshine blessed every moment's play.

Of the Bradman innings he wrote:
Woodfull and Ponsford began Australia's innings with grim, protective vigilance. Australia's score reached 100 just after lunch; the time of the day was half past two. At a quarter past three the score was 150 for none, Ponsford 77, Woodfull 70. It was at this point in proceedings that King George came to Lord's and was presented on the field of play to the cricketers. From the first over after the King's departure from the scene, bowled by J.C. White, Ponsford was caught by Hammond in the slips. He 'followed' a wide ball. There is no doubt that Ponsford's wicket should really have gone to His Majesty's credit. At half past three when Australia were 162 for 1, Bradman walked to the wicket, taking his time. He drove his first ball smack to long off and when he had finished the stroke, he was near enough to the bowler to see the surprised look on White's face, for until this minute no batsman had dreamed of running out to drive White; in fact several very famous English cricketers had assured me that to drive White on the half volley was an

act scarcely comprehensible in terms of skill or common sanity. The advent of Bradman on this Saturday of a burning English summer was like the throwing of combustible stuff on fires that had been slumbering with dreadful potentiality. Nearly every ball was scored from. Bradman ran yards out of his ground to White and belaboured him; White was obliged to pitch short and then Bradman cut him to ribbons. After tea a massacre, nothing less. Never before this hour, or two hours until the close of play, and never since, has a batsman equalled Bradman's cool deliberate murder or spifflication of all bowling. Boundaries everywhere - right and left and in front. The bowler was helpless and at Bradman's mercy even as he ran to bowl. He reached 100 in one hour and three quarters, with 13 fours. At 5.20 Australia's score was 300 for 1; at 5.30 it passed 350. Tate was wildly cheered when he sent down a maiden to Bradman. But the England attack was entirely at a loss; not to get Bradman out - that wild hope had gone long since - but just to stem the flood of his

boundaries. There were not enough fieldsmen available; Bradman found gaps and vacancies in nature. Ten minutes before half past six, Woodfull was stumped pushing out to Robins's spin; and it is a mistake to think that he was a dull, unlovely batsman. His stiff arms and short lift-up of the bat distracted the attention of casual onlookers from the prettiness of his footwork. It was a compliment to Woodfull that he did not sink into anonymity, or invisibility even, while Bradman at the other end of the wicket played the most brilliant and dramatically incisive and murderous innings of his career, and played it without turning a hair. At half past six Australia's total was 404 for two; and Bradman, in little more than two hours and a half, had made 155, not once exerting himself, every shot dead in the target's middle, precise and shattering; an innings which was beautiful and yet somehow cruel in its excessive mastery.

As the cricketers came from the field, the light of a glorious June afternoon shone on them; it shines on them yet. A victory in four days won in the face of a total of 425; England though needed 304 to save defeat by an innings and though down and out at noon on the last day, in the fourth innings of a dusty Lord's wicket, forced Australia to sweat and strain at the finish. It was the match of everybody who played in it. Victor and vanquished emerged with equal honour; and the chief laurel crowned the fair perspiring brow of A.P.F. Chapman. The match of every cricketer's heart's desire.

- *Cardus in the Covers,*
  by Sir Neville Cardus, 1978.

Chapman tries, unsuccessfully, to stop a Bradman cut past point during his innings of 254 in the Second Test at Lord's. Duckworth is the wicket-keeper. At that time, it was the highest score ever made at Lord's and the highest Test score ever in England. In an ABC radio interview after his retirement, Sir Donald said that, technically, it was the best innings he ever played. Asked to nominate the best innings of his career, Sir Donald replied:

In terms of sheer technical satisfaction perhaps my 254 at Lord's in 1930, simply because with one or two exceptions every ball went exactly where I intended it to go. I suppose my scores of 452 in Sydney and 334 at Leeds [see pages 56 to 61] must rank highly, but I made errors in them, and from a team viewpoint neither was as important as perhaps my 173 not out at Leeds in 1948 [see page 238], which helped bring a rather historic and unexpected victory. It gave me much satisfaction because of its value to the side and because of the batting difficulties I had to overcome in that innings. And the same applies to my century in Melbourne in the 1932-1933 series. But there is not much personal satisfaction in making a hundred and being missed several times. Any artist must surely aim at perfection, and that is why I think Lord's, 1930, is my first choice. It was the nearest I could ever hope to get to such a goal.

Autographing cricket bats occupied many hours of Bradman's time. The nature of the task is indicated here by the pile of bats awaiting his signature at William Sykes Ltd's factory during the 1930 tour. During the 1934 tour Bradman once autographed 3,500 bats in one day.

Below: A 1930 photograph of Bradman showing his famous stance.

The day this photograph was taken, and the following day, turned out to be the most remarkable of Bradman's long career when he broke R.E. Foster's world record Test score of 287, with an inspired innings of 334, which included 309 on the first day. He made 105 before lunch, 115 between lunch and tea, and 89 between tea and stumps, a performance almost beyond description and, so far, unparalleled in Test cricket history.

Left: Going out to bat on the first day of the Third Test at Leeds in July, 1930.

This photograph of Bradman resting beside the pitch during a drinks break at Leeds in 1930 shows another fascinating and genteel side of English Test cricket of the era. Note the waiter and waitress, complete with cap, serving the drinks.

Wicket-keeper George Duckworth throws the ball into the air after
finally catching Bradman for 334 off Maurice Tate.

Left: George Duckworth, who said on his
retirement from first-class cricket:
"This was the greatest innings I ever saw."

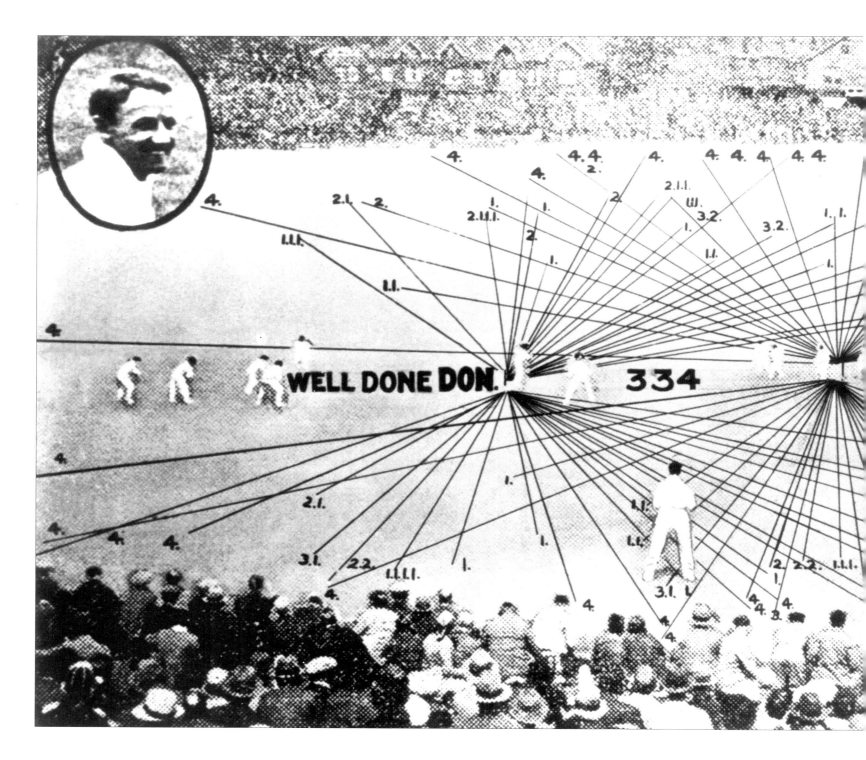

The scoring wheel of Bradman's record innings of 334 at Leeds. Compiled by the official Australian scorer, Mr W. Ferguson, it shows Bradman's amazing array of shots to all parts of the ground. Yorkshireman, Len Hutton, was to break the record in 1938, with a score of 364, but there was little to compare with Bradman's innings. Bradman's 334 was made in an incredible 383 minutes [six hours and 23 minutes]. Hutton took more than 13 hours. Bradman hit a Test record 46 fours.

"Bradman's batting today was almost indescribable. I was sitting with the Yorkshire Cricket Committee in the pavilion, listening to appreciation of Bradman's splendid innings. When Larwood bowled ineffectively at Bradman, P.F. Warner turned round to Lord Hawke and said: 'This is like throwing stones at Gibraltar'."

- A report by Arthur Mailey, former Australian Test cricketer and author, writing on Bradman's 309 not out on the first day of the Leeds Test.

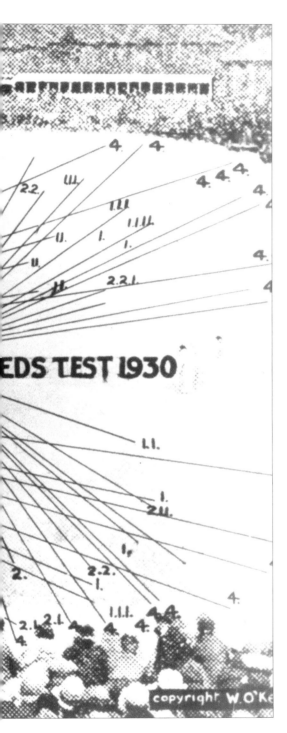

Surrounded by a cheering Leeds crowd on his way back to the pavilion
following his record-breaking innings. Bradman was then aged only 21.
Writing in *The Bradman Albums* he said:

•*In a long career there are many outstanding memories but I suppose the
opening day of the Third Test at Leeds
must rank as the greatest in my cricketing life. To break the world's record Test
score was exciting. To do so against*

*Australia's oldest and strongest rival
was satisfying. More than anything else,
however, was the knowledge that I had
scored the runs at such a fast rate and
therefore provided entertainment for the
spectators.*•

The Fourth Test at Manchester in July, 1930, was drawn due to rain. On the non-playing Sunday, Bradman met the great Ranjitsinhji for the first time when the Australians were lunch guests at the home of Sir Edwin Stockton, photographed here with some of his guests.
Back Row – The Hon. S.M. Bruce, W.Kelly [team Manager], Lt. Col. H.H. Shri Sir Ranjitsinhji Vibhaji [Ranji], W.M. Woodfull, W. H. Ponsford, W. Ferguson [scorer], A. Jackson, A. Hurwood and E.L. a'Beckett.
Front Row – C.V. Grimmett, W.A. Oldfield, D.G. Bradman, Lady Stockton, Sir Edwin Stockton, Mrs S.M. Bruce, C.W. Walker and T.W. Wall.

The great Ranji..

Signing a cricket bat before a set of tennis at Sir Edwin's home.

Practising before play in the Fifth Test at The Oval, London, in August, 1930.

It became an historic Test for a number of reasons. Australia scored a handsome victory by an innings and 39 runs and regained the Ashes. Bradman continued his supremacy over the England bowlers with yet another double century, an innings of 232. There was a memorable, record 243 fourth-wicket partnership between Bradman and Archie Jackson. And, although Bradman disputes the theory, many believe the events during the Test gave birth to "bodyline". [See pages 65, 105, 107 to 114].

Archie Jackson [left], and Bradman on the way to the wicket on the third day of the rain-interrupted Fifth Test. They weren't separated until one o'clock the following day when Jackson was caught Sutcliffe, bowled Wyatt for 73 and the partnership had yielded a record 243 for the fourth wicket.

During their record-breaking innings, both Bradman and Jackson received painful hits from Harold Larwood "bumpers". Arthur Mailey wrote that Bradman's performance under the prevailing conditions stamped him as "*the greatest batsman of all time*". Larwood claimed years later that Bradman's reactions to playing the short-pitched ball in this match were the genesis of the "bodyline" plan, used so successfully against the Australians in 1932-1933.

Left: Police keep spectators back as Bradman and Jackson head for the pavilion at the end of the third day.

Arthur Mailey and Bradman, taken in the 1950s.

Mailey in his early playing days.

Hitting to leg during his record partnership with Archie Jackson.

Cutting Larwood through slips to reach his century.

The Fifth Test was the last played by the legendary English batsman, Jack Hobbs. Sadly for spectators and players alike, Hobbs cut a ball from Alan Fairfax onto his wicket and was out for only nine. Sir Donald recorded in *Farewell to Cricket*:

'I wanted to see him make a good score on his final appearance. I didn't know in 1930 that Jack Hobbs' nine runs would be nine more than I was going to make in my final appearance on the same ground [18 years later].'

Bradman acknowledging the crowd on completing his first century at The Oval. Jack Hobbs is the player applauding in the background.

67

A rare mistimed shot as the ball kicks on a difficult pitch.

Maurice Tate, one of the England bowlers who felt the sting of Bradman's bat.

Bradman reached his double century on the fourth day of The Oval Test, although not without some anxious moments on a difficult pitch. In this shot the ball had spun into the air after Bradman mistimed a glance off Tate. Wicket-keeper Duckworth lunged, but the ball fell safely. Duckworth later figured in Bradman's controversial dismissal, caught behind for 232 off Harold Larwood. Bradman said he didn't believe he'd snicked the ball. In the Test, Bradman contributed nearly one-third of Australia's total of 695. England batted twice for 656 runs and were defeated by an innings and 39 runs. In *The Bradman Albums*, Sir Donald wrote of his performance:

•My own double century in the Fifth Test was made under somewhat difficult batting conditions and in some ways was the most valuable one of the series.•

Bulletin boards were widely used to help Australians keep up with the cricket scores in the days before direct radio broadcasts. This more unusual example was giving the latest from The Oval game of 1930.

Above: Among those to see Bradman's 232 in the Fifth Test was his friend from Bowral, Alf Stephens, who had travelled to England with his wife for the 1930 tour. This photograph shows Bradman's hand waving through the roof of the car to Alf, who is waving back with a handkerchief, just past the nose of the grey police horse.

Left: Mr and Mrs Alf Stephens with Bradman at the home of William Sykes, head of the famous English cricket bat manufacturing company with whom Bradman had a contract.

Left Below: Alf Stephens and Don photographed at Stoke during the 1930 tour.

A portrait taken on his 22nd birthday, August 27, 1930, a week after the Fifth Test.

With his faithful Royal typewriter.

Answering letters from well-wishers became part of his life during the 1930 England Tour. He continued to receive huge amounts of mail right throughout his cricketing career, and beyond. Keith Miller recalls that during the 1948 England Tour Bradman needed assistance to open all his letters, but insisted on personally answering as many as time permitted, especially those from children.

Above: Walter Lindrum, the world's greatest billiard player, gives some tips in London shortly before the end of the 1930 tour, not that Bradman needed much coaching. As in other ball games, he excelled in billiards and snooker. The photograph shows why one of Bradman's early nicknames was *"Goldie"*, referring to the colour of his hair. In later years, friends often called him *"Braddles"*.

Right: A publicity shot with actress Joyce Kennedy taken during the Australian team's visit to the Elstree Studios in September, 1930.

A portrait taken during the 1930 tour.

Bradman hits out of a bunker during the 1930 England Tour.

During the 1930 tour Bradman scored 3,170 runs in all matches at an average of 99.09. Bill Woodfull was next among the Australian batsmen with 1,568 runs at 58.07. In the traditional last match of the tour v Mr H.D.G. Leveson-Gower's XI at Scarborough, Bradman scored 96. The match also marked the last first-class appearance of another great English player, Wilfred Rhodes, who subsequently joined the ranks of those who considered Bradman to be *"the greatest batsman of all time"*.

The Bradman Albums contain Bradman's own thoughts on the success of the 1930 tour:

'The final Test played at The Oval … was the culmination of a hard series in which our young team, under the inspiring leadership of Bill Woodfull, moulded into a fine combination. We were given little chance at the outset by the critics, but the Australian players improved far more rapidly than had been anticipated. .. The whole tour was a wonderful experience and certainly laid the foundation for the balance of my career.'

As always, a study of concentration before playing this shot out of the short rough during a farewell golf game just before the 1930 tourists left England.

By the end of the 1930 tour of England, the young Don Bradman was being hailed as greater than the English cricketing legend, W.G. Grace, seen here with his sons, W.G. Grace Jr. [left] and C.B. Grace [right]. Amongst the odd souvenirs Bradman collected during his life in cricket was a cheque, payable to Dr W. G. Grace and endorsed by him. It was banked in 1907, the year before Bradman was born. In *Farewell to Cricket* Bradman said it was the only autograph he ever kept, apart from those on official team photographs.

Above and Left: Australia's Victor Trumper demonstrates the drive. Trumper and the Englishman, Jack Hobbs, were two of the other batting legends with whom Bradman was being compared right through the 1930s.

After the triumphant 1930 England Tour, Bradman returned to Australia to a hero's welcome, including a series of receptions organised by General Motors and his employers, the Sydney sports store, Mick Simmons Ltd. Bradman was suddenly swept along in a tide of blazing publicity over which he had no control. This mass display of public adoration gave the unfortunate impression that Bradman had won back the Ashes almost single-handed.

Jealousies and criticisms, some of which smouldered for years, emerged. At the same time he'd been reported to the Board of Control for alleged contractual breaches involving the publication in England of a newspaper series taken from his first book. The newspaper had undertaken not to publish the series while the tour was in progress, but broke the agreement. Bradman was not at fault, but the Board withheld £50 of his allowance. All of these events placed enormous new pressures on him for the 1930-1931 season and matches against the West Indies team on their inaugural visit to Australia. He wrote later he was in a *"disturbed state of mind"* for the start of the West Indies tour. Despite this, he scored a century and double century in the Tests , averaging 74.50. He averaged 115.83 in eight Sheffield Shield games. He also played a string of second-class matches, averaging 89.30 for all matches for the season.

On stage in Perth at the first of the huge "welcome home" receptions on the return of the 1930 team from England.

The automobile company, General Motors, and his employers, the Sydney sports store, Mick Simmons Ltd., staged a series of "welcome home" receptions for Bradman in Perth, Adelaide, Melbourne, Bowral and, finally, Sydney. This snapshot shows the first reception in Perth, where Bradman and members of the triumphant 1930 touring party were introduced on stage at the Theatre Royal.

At the wheel during his Adelaide motorcade.

From Perth, the team travelled by the Transcontinental railway to Adelaide, where Bradman was whisked away for a motorcade through the city streets. Accompanied by Mick Simmons' Publicity Manager, Oscar Lawson, he is seen here driving the leading car from the city centre to Adelaide's Parafield Airport, where a specially chartered Australian National Airways tri-motor plane, the *Southern Cloud*, was waiting to fly him to Melbourne and then to Goulburn. After Adelaide, he proceeded ahead of the rest of the team, at his employers' request. This early departure became contentious because it focused more public attention on Bradman, who later wrote:

•*No question of refusing entered my head because my employers had the perfect right to seek my return at the earliest possible moment.*•

He said he didn't realise the publicity, over which he had no control, would create an *"unfortunate impression"* until after the damage had been done.

The Don Bradman Special.

General Motors presented him with the Don Bradman Special, a red Chevrolet roadster, in honour of his deeds during the 1930 tour of England. He was handed the keys at a reception in Sydney. While Australians generally applauded the idea of the gift, it transpired that singling out Bradman for reward resulted in further unfair and unwarranted criticisms about the extent of personal publicity after his English triumphs.

Bradman, wearing a hat and overcoat, is on the right of Pilot T.W. Shortridge, captain of the chartered ANA plane, *Southern Cloud*. The photograph was taken shortly before the plane left Essendon Airport for Goulburn. Flying was still a hazardous adventure in the early 1930s because it was well before the days of electronic navigational aids. An indication of this was the late arrival of the *Southern Cloud* on the earlier flight from Adelaide when Captain Shortridge strayed off course. A few months later the *Southern Cloud* vanished with passengers and crew. Its disappearance remained one of Australia's greatest aviation mysteries until 1958 when the plane's wreckage was found in the Australian Alps.

Above: Ready to board the *Southern Cloud* for the flight from Melbourne to Goulburn.

Right: Capt. Shortridge. Bradman joined him in the cockpit.

Leaving Goulburn Airport.

The famous racing driver, Wizard Smith, and Bradman's brother, Vic, were at Goulburn to meet the *Southern Cloud*. They are photographed [left] ready for the next stage of Bradman's whirlwind return, the short road trip home to Bowral, where hundreds turned out to give him a hero's welcome home. The well-wishing went late into the night. Bradman, normally an early riser, slept in the next morning and Wizard Smith had to drive at speeds of up to 82 mph to get Bradman from Bowral to a Sydney reception on time. While called on to speak at public functions, Bradman, to his credit, did nothing to fuel the fires of unwanted personal publicity by declining to make any newspaper comment about himself or the tour. One newspaper suggested it was unusual for a prominent Australian to return from abroad and decline to talk. Bradman replied:

It is not unusual with me; I have not given anything to a newspaper since I landed.

Father, son and brother reunited. Left to right, Vic, Don and George Bradman.

Addressing hundreds of well-wishers on his return to Bowral.

Above: A mother greets her son. A touching scene as Don Bradman and Mrs Emily Bradman embrace on Bradman's return home to Bowral at the end of his triumphant 1930 tour of England.

Right: Bradman presents his mother with a bouquet of flowers.

Jessie Menzies, soon to be Mrs Don Bradman, poses on the bumper bar of the new red Chevrolet, presented to Bradman by General Motors. The photograph was taken at the Bradman home in Glebe Street, Bowral.

Don and Jessie during their courting days in 1931. Don had proposed before the start of the 1930 tour, but Jessie suggested they wait until he returned to see if they still felt the same. They did and were married in Burwood, Sydney, in April the following year, 1932.

Don and Jessie Bradman in 1931.

A promotional shot of Bradman after he had become internationally famous.

The NSW Sheffield Shield side for the southern tour matches against Victoria and South Australia in 1930.

Back Row– S.J. McCabe, H.S. Love, H. Hooker, G. Stewart, O.W. Bill, J. Fingleton, W. Hunt.
Front Row– D.G. Bradman, A.A. Jackson, A.F. Kippax [Captain], F. Buckle [Manager], H.C. Chilvers, A.G. Fairfax.

O. Wendell Bill

Bradman played six Shield innings in 1930-1931, scoring 61, 121 and 258 against South Australia and 2, 33 and 220 against Victoria. He said later his 220 against Victoria gave him the most pleasure because of a record fifth-wicket partnership of 234 in 135 minutes with O. Wendell Bill, who later became a close friend. The following season they were to figure in another historic partnership, in a second-class match at Blackheath where Bradman scored 100 runs in three overs [see page 93].

West Indies fast bowling trio Griffith, Constantine and Francis.

By Bradman's own assessment, his form against the West Indies was *"patchy"* partly due to staleness, a common problem among first-class players returning from an England tour because the "home" season becomes the third without a long break. In the Tests, he scored 4, 25, 223,152, 43 and, in the Fifth and final Test, his first duck in Test cricket. Although the West Indies at that time were, in Bradman's mind, not quite up to international standard, they had some world class players, among them George Headley, their star batsman, and fast bowlers [above] H.C Griffith, L. Constantine and G.N. Francis.

When he wrote *Farewell to Cricket* in 1950, Bradman then rated Constantine *"without hesitation the greatest all-round fieldsman"* he had ever seen.

The West Indian all-rounder Learie Constantine batting in the SCG nets.

He was out for a duck, bowled H.C. Griffith in the second innings of the Fifth Test against the West Indies at the Sydney Cricket Ground in March, 1931. Australia lost the Test by 30 runs, although they won the series 3-1. Bradman later wrote of the West Indies bowling attack:

In the bowling line they badly lacked a top-grade spinner, but in Griffith, Francis and Constantine they had a trio of fast bowlers quite up to Test standard.

The camera catches one of his rare ducks in Test cricket.

George Headley.

The young George Headley, the West Indian star bat, is on the left in this rare archival photograph. With him are Sealey [centre] and Hunte.

Above: Bradman was a talented musician. His skills as a pianist were often in demand, particularly on the long sea voyages to England and Canada. In this 1934 photograph he is entertaining A.G. Chipperfield [left] and L. O'B. Fleetwood-Smith.

With the famous 1930s musician Jack Lumsdaine, recording a Lee Sims arrangement for the piano.

Recording "Every Day is a Rainbow Day for Me", in 1930.

Music has given Bradman enormous pleasure. Apart from being an accomplished pianist, one of his musical compositions "Every Day is a Rainbow Day for Me" was recorded by Columbia Records. He is shown here during the recording session at Columbia's Homebush studios in Sydney. He autographed the wax record.

Left: The sheet music for "Every Day is a Rainbow Day for Me".

A rare photograph of Bradman ready to bat for NSW.

Stan McCabe and Bradman going out to bat for NSW against Victoria at the Sydney Cricket Ground in 1931.

One of his regrets in 1930-1931 was his failure, through injury, to see an extraordinary innings by his NSW and Australian team mate, Stan Mc-Cabe. Bradman and McCabe accompanied an Alan Kippax team on a Northern Queensland tour at the end of the 1930-1931 first-class season. However, Bradman badly sprained his right ankle while fielding in a match at Rockhampton, an injury which he believes weakened it and probably con-tributed to a more serious mishap at The Oval in 1938, and another in the last first-class match of his career in 1949. He spent 18 days recovering in Rockhampton Hospital. The McCabe innings he regretted not seeing was played soon after at Gympie when McCabe hit 18 sixes in a score of 173. Bradman, who had great admiration for McCabe, said:

That must have been worth watching.

Just before the start of the 1931-1932 season Bradman became the centre of yet another unwarranted controversy, this time over an offer for him to play as a professional with the Accrington Club in the English Lancashire League. There was a public outcry, which a newspaper of the day described as *"pitiful wails"* and *"sheer stupidity"*, saying that trying to force Bradman to stay in Australia was like fining him for *"eating the fruits of his own genius"*. Ultimately, Bradman refused the offer after accepting a writing and promotions contract from Associated Newspapers Ltd., Radio 2UE Ltd. and F.J. Palmer and Son Ltd., little realising at the time the contract would lead to future controversy. Bradman said the whole episode, which subjected him to conflicting emotions and opinions, had further *"disturbed my peace of mind"*. When the season finally started, he played his sole Test series against South Africa. It proved to be the most successful Test series of his career. His Test aggregate of 806 and average of 201.5 against the South Africans speak for themselves.

Another classic Bradman stroke, sweeping for four in a club match for St. George against Gordon. Note the perfect finishing position and how the wrists have been rolled over the top of the bat to keep the ball along the ground.

Bradman turned out for his Sydney first-grade club, St. George, as often as representative duties allowed from 1926 right through to 1933 when residential qualifications forced him to play for North Sydney. This photograph was taken during one of his most memorable club innings of 1931-1932, against Gordon at Chatswood Oval. The wicket-keeper is Bert Oldfield. He scored 201 in 171 minutes. The second century took only 45 minutes. In *Farewell to Cricket*, Bradman said he remembered it well because he hit a six over point from a half volley, only to be told by a fieldsman it was a mishit. He added:

•For his benefit I nominated this shot and repeated it later on, but must add it could hardly be done except on a small ground like Chatswood.•

Two greats together, Bradman and Charles Macartney.

This rare photograph from Sir Donald's personal collection has particularly fond memories for him. It was taken at Chatswood Oval in Sydney, during a St. George-Gordon first-grade club match, probably on the same day as the photograph on the previous page.

It is unusual and historic because it was one of the few ever taken of Bradman wearing his St. George club blazer and the only photograph ever taken of him and Macartney together in club blazers. Macartney, who played for Gordon, had retired from Test cricket in 1926.

Bradman's first match against South Africa was for NSW at the SCG in November, 1931. He scored an indifferent 30 in the first innings and a brilliant 135 in 128 minutes in the second. When the teams met again the following month, he was in devastating form, scoring 219 in 234 minutes. The photograph on the right was taken during that innings. He was eventually caught off McMillan's bowling. In the Tests against South Africa, Bradman showed almost complete mastery over the visitors with scores of 226, 112, 2, 167 and 299 not out, for an average of 201.5, his most successful ever Test series.

Again in classic pose, off-driving the South African slow bowler, Q. McMillan.

South Africa's Captain, H.B. Cameron, who left an outstanding impression on Bradman for his shrewd captaincy and playing skill.

South African batsmen F.H. Curnow [left] and H.W. Taylor resume their innings against NSW at the Sydney Cricket Ground in 1931.

The South African fast bowler, A.J. Bell, [left] bowled to Bradman in seven matches, often for hours on end, without taking his wicket. Bell was with cricket writer, A. G. Moyes, when Bradman walked in for a chat. As Bradman left, Bell said in a voice resonant with admiration: *"That's the first time on this tour I've seen his back."* Bell said that when batting Bradman always seemed to assume *"a sort of cynical grin, which reminds me of the Sphinx"*. He said South Africans were under the impression Bradman was only a great forward player. He said: *"This is quite erroneous. He is the finest back player any of us have ever seen."*

In December, 1931, Bradman performed one of his most amazing feats by scoring 100 runs in three eight-ball overs during a match to mark the opening of a new malthoid pitch at Blackheath in the Blue Mountains, near Sydney. In this rare photograph Bradman [centre] and the Mayor of Blackheath, Peter Sutton [on Bradman's left], are preparing to cut the ribbon at the opening. Bradman and NSW player,

O. Wendell Bill, standing on Bradman's right, were guest players for Blackheath in a match against neighbouring Lithgow. Mid-way through his innings of 256, Bradman walked down the pitch and said to Wendell Bill: "*I think I'll have a go.*" He did. Bradman scored 100 runs off the next 22 balls he faced. Wendell Bill scored two off the other two balls. Bradman's total of 256 included 14 sixes and 29 fours. He hit

10 of the sixes and nine of the fours during his century scoring spree.

Here are the scoring shots that made up Bradman's 100 runs and Wendell Bill's two, the latter scored in turning over the strike to Bradman on the first and fifth balls of the third over:
First over: 6 6 4 2 4 4 6 1
Second over: 6 4 4 6 6 4 6 4
Third over: 1 6 6 1 1 4 4 6

Bradman and the Mayor of Blackheath, Peter Sutton, prepare to open the new pitch.

The bat Bradman used is on display at Blackheath Bowling Club, which adjoins the ground. In a taped message to the club, Sir Donald said:

It is important, I think, to emphasise that the thing was not planned. It happened purely by accident and everyone was surprised at the outcome, no one more so than I.
I don't know whether my 100 in three overs is a record. All I can say is I never heard of anything similar. Wendell Bill became one of my staunchest friends and, in later years, said he got more notoriety out of the two singles scored in those three overs than anything else he ever did in his life.

The match had another special memory for Bradman. At a post-match dinner, Lithgow player, coalminer, Bob Nicholson, was asked to sing. Bradman was so impressed by his glorious baritone voice he invited Nicholson to sing at his wedding to Jessie Menzies the following year. Nicholson went on to become a famous opera singer. Sir Donald said:

There was a hushed crowd at the wedding and Jessie said afterwards that the congregation was more excited about the singing than the wedding. A century in three overs and the start of a magical musical career for a Lithgow coalminer. What a day!

Broadcasting on Sydney radio station 2UE.

The contract signed at the end of 1931 to end the controversy about his tempting professional offer from England involved Bradman in regular broadcasts on Sydney radio 2UE. This photograph, taken in 1932, shows him giving one of his early radio talks from 2UE's Sydney studios.

Aboriginal speedster, Eddie Gilbert, throws his hands in the air as he has Bradman caught behind the wicket for 0.

Lightning-fast Eddie Gilbert.

In Sheffield Shield matches in 1931-1932, Bradman had an unusual sequence of scores, 0, 23, 167, 23 and 0. The first duck was against Queensland when caught by Waterman off an Eddie Gilbert thunderbolt. Gilbert, the Aboriginal speedster, generated bewildering pace despite a shuffling run-up of only a few steps. His chances of Test selection were hindered by inconsistent form and a suspect bowling action. He occasionally appeared to bend his arm. His first-class career ultimately ended when umpire George Borwick consistently no-balled him for his action. Bradman recalled in *Farewell to Cricket* that one delivery from Gilbert *"knocked the bat out of my hand"*. He added:

I unhesitatingly class this short burst as faster than anything seen from Larwood or anyone else.

Bradman had good reason to remember the Fifth Test against South Africa because of what he called in *Farewell to Cricket* "an incredible" happening:

•*Grimmett and I were both in the Australian team. I did not bat and Grimmett did not bowl.*

Bradman didn't bat because of an ankle injury suffered when he jumped off a form in the dressing room. Grimmett wasn't needed. South Africa were dismissed for 36 in the first innings and 45 in the second, with Bert Ironmonger capturing 11 of the wickets for 24 runs.

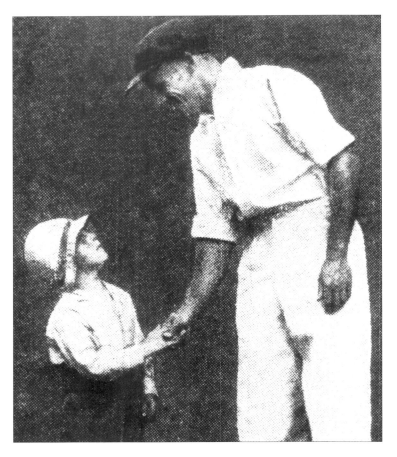

Right: A delightful moment as he shakes hands with a very young admirer during the Fifth Test against the touring South Africans in Melbourne in February, 1932.

One of Bradman's pastimes was wrestling. He went regularly to the Olympia Gymnasium in Sydney to improve his knowledge of the sport. It also helped his strength and fitness.

Right: Demonstrating a reverse headlock on amateur middleweight wrestling champion, Jim Deakin.

Jessie Menzies made a stunning bride when she married Don Bradman at St. Paul's Church, Burwood, Sydney, on April 30, 1932. Here, the happy couple pose after the wedding ceremony.

The bridal party after the wedding.
Left to right: The best man, Vic Bradman, Don Bradman, Jessie Bradman,
Jessie's sisters, Jean and Lily Menzies, and brother, Roy Menzies.

During the 1931-1932 Australian season Bradman's old acquaintance and former Test player, the ebullient Arthur Mailey, dreamed up an ambitious scheme to take a touring team to Canada and the USA at the end of the season, but sponsors made it contingent that Bradman be in the side. Bradman finally agreed when arrangements were made for his new bride, Jessie, to accompany him, thereby turning the trip into an extended honeymoon. It was mainly a goodwill tour. Despite playing against much weaker teams, frequently numbering 15 or 18 players to even up the odds, the tour was both successful and highly enjoyable for all, even though towards the end Bradman was feeling *"off colour"* due partly to the stress of playing too much cricket. He played in all 51 matches on the tour, scoring 3,782 runs, with 14 not outs, a highest score of 260 and an average of 102.1. The team included Test players Richardson, McCabe and Kippax.

The Arthur Mailey team to tour the USA and Canada in 1932.

Back Row– P. Carney, K. Tolhurst, E. Rofe, W. Ives, L. O'B. Fleetwood-Smith, S. McCabe.
Second Row– D.G. Bradman, V. Richardson [Captain], A. Mailey, A. Kippax.
Front Row– H. S. Carter, R. Nutt.

The happy honeymoon couple with the Captain of the steamer SS *Niagara*, which took the team to Canada.

Waving goodbye on board ship.

Don and Jessie in a delightfully informal pose in Stanley Park, Vancouver.

Mailey's XI played their first match on Vancouver Island. Their opponents, a Cowichan Club team, batted 18 players to equalise the odds, but were still trounced. They made 194. The Australians replied with 503 for 8, in the process hitting the ball so far so often that six balls were lost in the surrounding shrubbery. Stan McCabe was the star with 150. Bradman scored 60.

A visit to Hollywood provided some of the most memorable moments of the tour. The party visited various movie studios and met famous stars of the day, among them Mary Astor, Jean Harlow, Maureen O'Sullivan, Myrna Loy, Boris Karloff, Ronald Colman and Leslie Howard. As the photo shows, Jessie Bradman also met up with the Australian actor, "Snowy" Baker, a keen polo player.

The Australian actor "Snowy" Baker [far left] introduces Jessie Bradman to his polo-playing friends in Hollywood.

While visiting "Snowy" Baker's stables, Jessie Bradman, a skillful horsewoman, took the opportunity to ride one of the local horses.

Don Bradman seems fascinated by this performing dog while waiting his turn to bat against an 18-man Hollywood team.

The English actor and former England Test Captain [1888-1889], Sir Charles Aubrey-Smith, led the Hollywood side. Boris Karloff, of *Frankenstein* fame, was one of Hollywood's best bats. There were two matches. The Australians won both, scoring 2 for 144 to Hollywood's 18 for 114 in the first and 2 for 182 in reply to Hollywood's 18 for 164 in the second. Bradman contributed 52 not out in the first match and 83 not out in the second. The dog in the photograph was owned by Jack Oakey, who played in the Hollywood team.

The Mailey team members were out-fitted in fashionable attire of the period, including boater hats. Sammy Carter, Australia's old-time wicket-keeper, standing on the extreme left of this photograph, ultimately lost sight in one eye as the result of being hit by a ball on tour when it flew off an uneven coir mat surface. There were some amazing performances during the tour, even if against inferior opponents. In Ottawa, Fleetwood-Smith, yet to make his name in the Test arena, took nine wickets for seven runs. There were many light-hearted moments. Bradman recalled that in one match in New York the square leg umpire wandered off to the boundary fence to chat to friends.

Bradman and some of the Mailey team members show off their straw boaters.

Right: Two champions, Bradman and the great US baseball player George Herman "Babe" Ruth, shake hands during a baseball game between the Yankees and the White Sox in New York. Bradman surprised Ruth with his knowledge of baseball. The "Babe", himself no giant, was equally surprised by Bradman's lack of size and weight, but remarked:

"Us little fellows can hit 'em harder than the big ones."

Bradman and Babe Ruth meet in 1932.

1932 - 1933

Bradman arrived back from the North American tour little realising the storm that lay ahead. The Englishmen, due to tour in 1932-1933 under Captain, Douglas Jardine, had been plotting Bradman's batting downfall, devising what was soon to become the most detested word in cricket: "bodyline". The tactic to bowl fast short-pitched deliveries at, rather than to, the batsman, aided by a packed leg-side field, was abhorred and widely condemned. Jardine's chief weapon was Harold Larwood. But even before a ball was bowled, Bradman had another fight on his hands, a bitter argument with the Board of Control over the newspaper contract he'd signed to keep him in Australia in 1931. The Board now ruled he couldn't write for newspapers and play Test cricket at the same time unless solely employed as a journalist. Already beset with health problems that were to cause him increasing difficulties in later years, Bradman revealed in *Farewell to Cricket:* "*You can imagine my mental state when this decision was conveyed to me.*" Yet again, a bitter public wrangle developed, due to no fault of Bradman's. The matter was finally resolved when the newspaper released Bradman from his writing contract. With his deteriorating health and the incessant arguments, Bradman's mental preparation for the tough season ahead was far from ideal. He started the season with a flash of brilliance, scourging Victoria's bowlers in a Sheffield Shield match, scoring 238 runs in 210 minutes. Then came bodyline. In the end, bodyline curbed Bradman's prolific scoring, but did not defeat or destroy him, as it did others. He still averaged 56.57 in the Tests, far ahead of any other Australian batsman.

As well as grappling with business and cricket problems, the newly-weds had domestic matters to attend to about the time this photograph [left] was taken in November, 1932. They moved into their first home, at McMahons Point, in Sydney, a happy occasion, but one which also ended Bradman's playing days with the St. George Club. Residential requirements forced him to switch to North Sydney at the end of the season.

Left: Don and Jessie Bradman soon after their return from North America.

Below: Photographed in Wellington, New Zealand.

Stretching for a shot on the tennis court in 1932.

While Bradman's life revolved around cricket, he didn't lose touch with his other sporting joy, tennis, which he played for both relaxation and fitness. He was fiercely competitive on the tennis court and played as often as time allowed, and many times against Davis Cup players of the day.

Alan McGilvray recalls playing against him in a social match in Adelaide. He later wrote:

"It became fairly obvious fairly quickly that Bradman did not like to come second in such contests. I could handle a tennis racquet reasonably well, and at that stage of my sporting life I was a fairly fit and agile youth. I won something like 6-4, 6-2. When Bradman was serious about something his eyes actually burned at you. I can remember the look in his eyes that day as we left the court. 'You won't do that again', he told me, not in a nasty way, but with the sort of grim determination that I later came to know to be the very hub of his nature. If I needed any convincing it came some time later, when we had another game. This time he whipped me. He played as if his life depended on it. He was a born winner."

- The Game Is Not The Same,
   Alan McGilvray with
   Norman Tasker, 1985.

Above: Jessie Bradman in the garden of their McMahons Point home with the recently completed Sydney Harbour Bridge in the background.

Another rare photograph, this time about to open the "dicky-seat" of a car outside the Sydney Cricket Ground during the First Test of the infamous bodyline series.

He was a spectator at the First Test due to illness. Watching from the stand, he was filled with admiration for McCabe's 187 against hostile bowling and was impressed by Larwood's tremendous speed and sustained accuracy. He later wrote:

In the second innings when Larwood took 5 for 28 in 18 overs, I think he bowled faster over a longer period than I can remember seeing from him or anybody else.

England won the match. Afterwards, he warned members of the Board of Control about the dangers posed by leg-theory, but his warning was ignored.

The photograph on the right shows the packed leg-side field, which England Captain, Douglas Jardine, employed in conjunction with short, rising deliveries aimed at the batsman's body. Bradman attempted to counter this by drawing away and trying to hit to the off side. Some critics claimed he did it mainly to avoid being hit, but as the most nimble-footed batsman in the Australian side he was in least danger from bodyline. In devising his unorthodox counter-tactics Bradman's main interest was scoring runs. He argued it would be better to attack to the off rather than fall into Jardine's trap of trying to score against bodyline to the leg, which he believed carried the near certainty of injury or early dismissal, neither of which would be in the team's interest. While not totally effective, Bradman had more success in countering bodyline than any other batsman. This included Stan McCabe, who had scored a gallant and brilliant 187 not out in the First Test. Bradman still averaged 56.57 for the series, the highest of any Australian batsman. As former NSW selector and author A.G. "Johnnie" Moyes wrote in his book, *Bradman*:

"It is fair to say that no other player in the game could have attempted what he [Bradman] did with any possible hope of success. The fact remains that Bradman scored more runs in four Tests than anybody else did in five. There was no real solution. Bradman at least went on making runs. His critics did not."

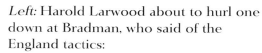

Left: Harold Larwood about to hurl one down at Bradman, who said of the England tactics:

Only those who have played against bodyline bowling are capable of understanding its dangers. I do not know of one batsman who has played against fast bodyline bowling who is not of the opinion that it will kill cricket.

Bradman batting against a "bodyline" field in the 1932-1933 series. Larwood is the bowler.

Douglas Jardine.

Harold Larwood.

Australian Captain, Bill Woodfull, ducks under a Harold Larwood "thunderbolt".

In the Second Test, Bradman made a famous first-ball duck, bowled Bowes, but made amends in the second innings with almost a lone hand of 103 not out, out of a total of 191. Australia won. In the infamous Third Test in Adelaide, the most unpleasant in Test history, the Australians felt the full fury of bodyline. Both Woodfull and Oldfield received severe blows, causing a near riot. Australia lost the match. Bradman scored 8 and 66.

Bill Woodfull reels after being hit in the chest by Larwood.

Bert Oldfield clutches at his head when struck by a Larwood bouncer.

Surrounded by well-wishers, Bradman arrives at Brisbane railway station prior to the Fourth Test.

He scored 76 and 24 in Brisbane. He was out both times trying to hit Larwood to the off side, in line with the counter-tactics he decided to employ against Larwood's short-pitched "leg theory" bowling. England won the Test and regained the Ashes.

While bodyline subdued Bradman, it had a demoralising effect on other Australian batting hopefuls, including Len Darling [left] and Leo O'Brien.

In his book *Bradman*, published in 1948, A.G. Moyes, described the bodyline season as *"the most tragic that Test cricket has ever known".*

"There was to be bitterness that passed all understanding: angry words between men who were normally peaceful citizens and lovers of cricket. Cables were to pass to and fro, cables which contained in them the dynamite that might at any moment blow into little pieces the great structure of international cricket. It all happened because of Bradman's genius. A new method of attack was devised to reduce him to the level of an ordinary mortal, a type of attack that was certain to - and that did - cause bodily harm to cricketers in what had up to then been a game of skill."

A.G. Moyes [left] and Bradman with an unidentified cricketer.

Walking down the pitch to assist McCabe who had taken a nasty blow on the shoulder from a short-pitched Larwood delivery in the Brisbane Test.

Bowled by Larwood, attempting to leg glance in the first innings of the Fifth Test at the Sydney Cricket Ground in February, 1933.

He had scored 48 in 71 minutes, in what was described as a brilliant, if sometimes reckless, innings against the fast leg-theory. Mid-way through the innings he reached another milestone, 3,000 runs in all Test matches. Larwood, who never played in another Test against Australia, remained unrepentant over the years about his role in bodyline. He said he'd been obeying his Captain's instructions and saw no reason to apologise. In his autobiography, *The Larwood Story*, co-written by Kevin Perkins and published in 1982, Larwood paid Bradman the ultimate tribute:

"He was the most challenging batsman I ever bowled to. I have no hesitation in saying Bradman is the greatest batsman in my lifetime. I doubt if there will ever be another like him."

Driving Verity in the Fifth Test.

Bradman's second innings in the Fifth Test was equally daring. He had all but mastered Larwood, only to be deceived, and bowled, by a Verity yorker for 71. In this famous shot, taken by the *Sydney Mail* photographer, Herbert Fishwick, he is shown driving Verity through the covers for four. England won the match by eight wickets.
One of England's greatest batsmen, Walter Hammond, condemned body-line in his book, *Cricket My Destiny*, and revealed he would have retired had it continued. He supported Bradman's views by saying:

"It constitutes an attack on the batsman which he can only avoid by risking serious injury or by getting out quickly. No one was killed by bodyline, but that was good luck rather than a normal average."

An extremely rare shot of Bradman because he carried the drinks very few times in his cricket career. The only official time in a Test was when he was relegated to 12th man for the Second Test against England in 1928. The last time was during the Fifth Test of the bodyline series in 1932-1933 when a blow on the arm from Larwood kept him off the field for a while and he helped out by carrying the drinks.

Carrying the drinks at the Sydney Cricket Ground in 1933.

Yards down the wicket driving Hammond during the 1932-1933 series. Les Ames is the wicket-keeper.

Bowled Mitchell in the NSW v MCC match at the
Sydney Cricket Ground in 1932-1933.

One of the last matches Bradman played for his Sydney club, St. George, was when he made a nostalgic return to Bowral for a social match against a local XI captained by his old friend, Alf Stephens. Bradman scored 154 and 71.

With his friend Alf Stephens inspecting the wicket at Loseby Park, Bowral.

Walking onto St Paul's Oval at Sydney University in 1932 when he played as a guest for an I Zingari XI against a St. Paul's College XI. On his right is NSW Sheffield Shield batsman, O. Wendell Bill. Bradman was run out for 15.

117

Bradman, photographed in 1932.

1933 - 1934

As it transpired, the 1933-1934 season was Bradman's last for NSW. In February, 1934, he notified the NSW Cricket Association he intended moving to South Australia to begin a new career with an Adelaide share broker, H.W. Hodgetts, thereby ending his dependence on sport as a means of livelihood. When the time came to leave the State of his birth, Bradman said he felt *"rather like a boy leaving home"*. He was continuing to feel the strain of *"playing, thinking and talking"* cricket, but put down his feelings of ill-health to overwork. There were no international fixtures. Bradman had another dazzling domestic season, scoring 2,571 runs in all first and second-class matches, at an average of 88.6. In the Sheffield Shield he scored 922 runs, had a top score of 253 and averaged 184.4 in seven visits to the crease. The season ended on a most satisfactory note with his appointment as Australian Vice-Captain to Bill Woodfull for the 1934 tour of England.

The NSW side selected to play Victoria in January, 1934.

Back Row – W.A. Brown, A.G. Chipperfield, C.J. Hill, H.J. Theak, W.J. O'Reilly, O.W. Bill, W.A. Oldfield.
Front Row – R. Rowe, D.G. Bradman, A.F. Kippax [Captain], J.H. Fingleton, H.C. Chilvers.

Despite ill health in the match against Victoria, Bradman was in devastating form after a slow start. He finished with 128 in only 96 minutes, the last 118 runs coming in only 58 minutes. The match was drawn.

One of the last photographs of him wearing his NSW cap.

He finished his NSW career in glorious fashion. He got off to a dazzling start in the 1933-1934 Sheffield Shield season with a score of 200 in 184 minutes in the opening match against Queensland, in Brisbane, and 187 not out and 77 not out against Victoria a few weeks later in the second. He followed this with 253 in Queensland's return match against NSW at the SCG. During this match, won outright by NSW, Bradman and Alan Kippax shared a record third-wicket partnership of 363.

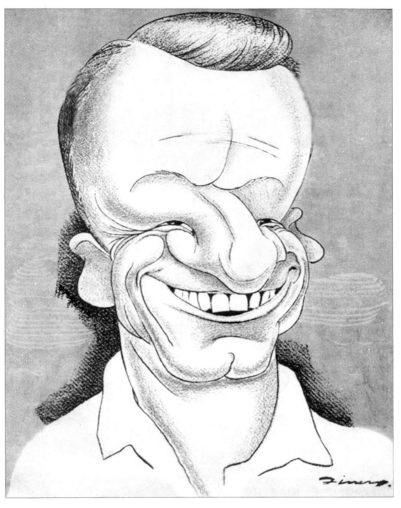

At the end of the 1933-1934 season Don and Jessie Bradman moved to Adelaide, where Bradman joined the sharebroking firm of Mr H.W. Hodgetts. Don and Jessie were photographed [below] at Mr Hodgetts' Adelaide home. His move to Adelaide before leaving on the 1934 England tour meant he would meet the three-months residential rule qualifying him to play for South Australia at the start of the 1934-1935 season. He wasn't to know then, but dramatic events later in the year were to delay those plans.

Left: A 1934 caricature of Bradman by cartoonist George Finey.

The cover of a brochure distributed to passengers aboard RMS *Orford* which carried the Australian cricketers to England.

Don and Jessie Bradman in Adelaide in 1934.

1934 England Tour

Bradman was still troubled with indifferent health at the start of the 1934 England Tour. As in 1930, he was in dazzling form in the first match against Worcestershire, again opening the tour with a double century, scoring 206. But only he knew the strain the effort had placed on him and, for a time, his game fell away. His friend and author, A. G. Moyes, years later described it as a period of *"brilliant uncertainties".* Bradman showed only flashes of the old genius. By the end of June he had scored only a modest, by his standards, 760 runs. It all changed after the Third Test. Bradman exploded back to life with 140 against Yorkshire, the century coming in 100 minutes. He then went on to score three centuries, a double century and a triple century in his next six innings. The season ended on an even more dramatic and unexpected note. Almost on the eve of the team's departure for home, Bradman suddenly fell ill. He underwent an emergency appendectomy and hovered close to death for several days with peritonitis. Jessie Bradman journeyed halfway across the world to be at his side. Bradman was considered lucky to have survived the ordeal.

The 1934 team for the tour of England. Bradman was appointed Vice-Captain.
In this montage, taken from the *Sydney Mail*, the caption under Bradman's photograph reads: "Greatest Batsman of Period".

Members of the 1934 team and Australian Davis Cup tennis players relax
on board the SS *Orford* during the voyage to England.

Sitting on the life boat - S. McCabe, B. Barnett.
Third row – L. Darling, A. Kippax, H. Ebeling, E.H. Bromley, W.A. Brown, L. Fleetwood-Smith, W. Ponsford, W. Oldfield, W. O'Reilly.
Second row – H. Bushby [Manager], Jack Crawford, W. Woodfull, A. Chipperfield, Don Bradman.
Front row – Don Turnbull, Viv McGrath, Adrian Quist, W.C. Bull [Treasurer], T. Wall.

Left: Bradman excelled in deck sports.
He is seen here playing deck quoits.

One of his early calls after arriving in England was on Mr William Sykes, the English cricket bat manufacturer. He is seen here having tea with Mr and Mrs Sykes at their home.

Apart from Douglas Jardine stating publicly he had *"neither the intention nor the desire"* to play cricket against the tourists, the welcome given to the Australians, including a personal welcome by the British Prime Minister, Mr Ramsay MacDonald, allayed concerns about any lingering ill will following bodyline. In *Farewell to Cricket*, Sir Donald wrote:

These spontaneous expressions of goodwill helped to dispose of any doubts regarding the reception we might anticipate following the turbulent summer of 1932-1933. The public very obviously wished to see cricket, and there was no hint of reserve in their enthusiasm.

Mayor of Southampton, Mr W.D. Buck, shakes hands with Bradman on the team's arrival at Southampton, England, on March 25, 1934.

Out, but with yet another double century at Worcester.

Bradman continues down the wicket after being bowled by R. Howorth in the traditional opening match of the 1934 tour against Worcestershire. As in 1930, he started the tour with a double century. He was finally out for 206. The innings placed a great strain on Bradman, who was feeling ill before the match and only played because of Bill Woodfull. He recalled in *Farewell to Cricket:*

•Woodfull persuaded me to play on the grounds that my withdrawal would lend colour to rumours about my unsatisfactory health and prove of psychological value to England. So I played, and, under considerable strain, steeled myself to see through an innings of 206. It was made in quick time and obtained a cordial press, but I was the only one aware of the drain on my resources. Indeed, it was largely as a result of this initial exertion that my cricket fell away.•

After some early disappointments, Bradman returned to his best against Middlesex just before the First Test. He played an innings of sheer majesty, scoring 160 in only 124 minutes. The innings evoked the tribute below from the English cricket writer, William Pollock.

Bradman drives H.J. Enthoven during the match.

BRADMAN SMITES MIDDLESEX
By William Pollock

AN INNINGS that thousands of us who love cricket are going to enshrine in our memories was played as the sun went down over Lord's on Saturday.

For more than forty years I have watched great batsmen - W.G., Ranji, Trumper, Frank Woolley, Macartney, Jessop, Hammond, Hobbs - and am grateful for many precious hours from them, but never have I seen a masterpiece of batting more glorious than Don Bradman's 100.

It was supreme, it was epic.

Le Don came in when the Middlesex's J. Smith [ex-Wiltshire] had got both Woodfull and Ponsford out for noughts with his village blacksmithy fast stuff, and for a ball or two he was not quite sure of himself. But the bit of luck that all batsmen need at the start was with him, and within five minutes the bowling was his toy.

His timing was marvellous, the power he got into his strokes extraordinary. Through the covers, straight past the bowlers, round to leg, down through the slips, the ball raced from his almost magic bat. All the shots were his, the whole field his kingdom. Smith's quickies, Walter Robins's slows, Ian Peebles' length ones, including an occasional googly, were just so much meat and drink to him.

> The ball no question made of ayes
>   or noes
> but right or left, as struck the
>   player went.

Le Don seemed to be inspired; he danced down the pitch and hit, he flung his left leg and drove, he lay back and pulled. I do not believe that any bowling in the world could have stopped the torrent of his run-making during this wonderful hour and a quarter. It was an honour to bowl and field during such an innings. It is no more than the frame of the picture to say that he put the ball to the boundary nineteen times, and that he got the one run he wanted for his hundred off the last ball of the evening.

Le Don has played the great innings of the season. If there is anything better to come from him or any one else, may I be there to see and share. The really great things of cricket are treasure.

In 1934 Jessie Bradman [second from the left] joined other Test cricket "widows" as guests of Sydney radio station 2BL to listen to cricket broadcasts from England. Because of technical limitations of the day, the short-wave broadcasts were unreliable and often very difficult to hear. These difficulties led to the introduction of special measures to bring the Test scores to a cricket-thirsty nation [see below].

This extremely rare photograph shows Sydney radio station 2BL's special cricket broadcasting studio in 1934. Commentators kept the nation informed via cables from England. They kept their own scoreboard - in this case showing the scores in the second innings of the drawn Third Test at Manchester. During the 1930s the ABC, under Charles Moses, pioneered the "synthetic" tests, where commentators used the cable information and special sound effects to give a realistic impression that their "ball by ball" descriptions were coming direct from England. Crowd noises were pre-recorded and a pencil tapped on wood was used to imitate bat on ball.

Returning to the pavilion after practice during the Second Test at Lord's.

After a convincing First Test win by 238 runs at Nottingham, Australia's luck ran out in the Second Test , played at Lord's, when beaten by a combination of rain and Hedley Verity, the Yorkshire left-hand bowler, who took 15 wickets in the match, including 8 for 43 in the second innings.

King George V shakes hands with Bradman during the Second Test, at Lord's.
At a previous meeting King George had remarked on The Don's strong handshake.

One of the most touching stories of the England tour emerged during the First Test in Nottingham, when Bradman saw a man looking through the gate, wistful and dejected. He was an unemployed Notts miner with scarcely a coin to his name and no hope of seeing the match. "Would you like to come in?" asked Bradman. In a matter of seconds the astonished man was inside the ground. Bradman paid his way, found him a place in the grandstand and gave him a few shillings to go on with. When it was discovered later that the miner, Herbert Elliott, had a wife and eight children, a subscription list was opened. Bradman headed it with a generous donation. The gesture was typical of Bradman's generosity both then and in later life.

Verity claimed Bradman's wicket in both innings of the Second Test, caught and bowled for 36 in the first and caught by wicket-keeper Ames for 13 in the second. Neville Cardus hailed Bradman's 36 as an innings verging on greatness. He wrote:

Let us thank fortune that Bradman got out when he did, on the crest of an innings of terrible power and splendour. For my part Bradman's innings of 36 this afternoon was far greater than his 334 at Leeds. Spirit lived in every stroke. It was an innings as safe and perfect in technique as any played by Trumper or J.T. Tyldesley.

Lifting Verity to the outfield in the Second Test at Lord's.

Back cutting Farnes past a lunging fielder at backward point in the Lord's Test. It went to the fence for four.

This skied mishit against Verity cost Bradman his wicket for 13 in the second innings
of the Second Test. Wicket-keeper Ames waits for and will finally take the catch,
watched by W.R. Hammond and H. Sutcliffe.

Australian Captain and Vice-Captain, Bill Woodfull
and Bradman, resume after the tea adjournment
against Somerset in 1934. Bradman was a
great admirer of Woodfull.

Bradman, was out for 17 in a following match against Somerset. At this stage of the tour he was still struggling with his form and his health. His poor state of health was never more obvious than during the drawn Manchester Third Test when he and Chipperfield, both afflicted by an infection called "Wimbledon Throat", left their sick beds to bat. Looking pale and thin, Bradman scored 30. An English cricket writer, who believed Bradman shouldn't have played, wrote:

"It may seem sloppy and sentimental to say so - and I have nothing to thank Bradman for - but I felt that I was pulling for him as he vainly strove to overcome insuperable obstacles. His was but the wraith of the greatness we once knew. The man is sick, and I would tear off an arm rather than say one hurtful word about him, but yesterday he reminded me of one who had thrown off his shroud to tilt at daunting cricketing windmills."

Almost as if waking from a bad dream, Bradman returned to his explosive best with 140 in 115 minutes against Yorkshire and carried this form into the crucial Fourth Test at Headingley a few days later, scoring 304 and sharing an Australian Test record fourth-wicket partnership of 388 with Bill Ponsford, who made 181. The pair are seen here [left], being escorted onto the field after the tea adjournment on the second day. Some critics rated Bradman's 304 a better innings than his record 334 on the same ground in 1930, although Bradman himself didn't regard it so.

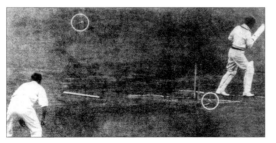

Above: Bradman hooks Lancashire left-arm bowler, Hopwood, on his way to a triple century in the Fourth Test.

Left: With stumps flying, he was finally bowled by W.E. Bowes in the Leeds Test. His innings included the first two sixes he ever hit in a Test in England.

His 304 and the record partnership with Ponsford were to no avail. Australia were in a winning position, when the match was abandoned because of rain and declared a draw. With the series level, only the Fifth Test remained to decide the Ashes. The tremendous strain of the long innings played havoc with Bradman's muscles. He wrote later:

Upon returning to our dressing room I was literally undressed by my team mates and carried to the massage table.

Right: Bradman returns to the pavilion after his innings of 304 at Leeds.

Right: His muscle problems surfaced again later that same day when he pulled a right thigh muscle chasing a hard drive from Hendren. Stan McCabe is seen here assisting him from the field. The injury was so severe it kept Bradman out of cricket for nearly a month.

A pull to leg during his record stand with Ponsford in the Fifth Test.

The Ashes-deciding Fifth Test at The Oval in 1934 proved to be another triumph for Bradman and Ponsford when they set a world and Test record second-wicket partnership of 451. Here, Bradman pulls while Ponsford starts to run. Ponsford scored 266 and Bradman 244, the second time in first- class cricket he'd made double centuries in successive innings.

Neville Cardus was among those who could scarcely believe the dual performance by Bradman and Ponsford. He wrote:

"If I were a writer of boy's fiction, I would not dare to make my heroes score 388 together in one match and 451 together in the next. The critics would tell me to keep my imagination within reasonable bounds."

Driving Hedley Verity in the Fifth Test at The Oval.

"Neville Cardus once asked Bradman what was his secret. 'Concentration. Every ball is for me the first ball, whether my score is 0 or 200.' And then he took my breath away by adding: 'And I never visualise the possibility of anybody getting me out'."
    - English cricket historian,
      H. S. Altham, 1941.

Right: Hedley Verity, the English left-arm spinner, one of the greatest of the world's cricketers to lose his life in World War II.

Bradman and Ponsford walk out to resume their
record-breaking partnership in the Fifth Test at The Oval.

Turning Bill Bowes past R.E.S. Wyatt at leg
during his record partnership with Bill Ponsford.

Bill Woodfull.

Bill Ponsford.

Their record 451 partnership helped
Australia to a massive first innings
total of 701, ensuring that Australia
won the Test, the rubber and the Ashes.
In *The Bradman Albums*, Bradman said
of the win:

*It was a fitting end to the captaincy of
Woodfull that he should lead Australia
to victory in his last Test. Though we
didn't know it at the time, this also
proved to be Ponsford's last Test, for he
retired at the end of the season.*

The Australians sprint from the field at the end of the Fifth Test. One player has already reached the gate. Bradman, cap in hand, leads the rest of the charge.

Australia had won the Fifth Test and the Ashes. In the two final tour matches Bradman provided some of the most thrilling cricket of the season, scoring 149 not out in 104 minutes, including 30 in a six-ball over, against an England XI at Folkestone. He then humbled a near-Test-strength bowling attack, scoring 132 in 90 hectic minutes against H.D.G. Leveson-Gower's XI at Scarborough, the last match of the tour. Bradman bracketed his innings at Scarborough with the one earlier in the season at Middlesex as the most exciting he ever played in England. Cricket writer, C.R.L. James, wrote the day after the Scarborough innings:

"After a shaky start... his excellences were multifarious and unique...The essence of any game is conflict, and there was no conflict here; the superiority on one side was too overwhelming. Bradman was 50 in 38 minutes and 100 in 80; then he started running out to Verity, and either drove him high to the on-boundary or along the ground past cover. He hit him for 19 runs in an over, and scored 32 in 10 minutes before he was stumped. There is not the slightest doubt that, had he wished, he could have continued to play quietly - that is to say, at a mere 80 per hour - and make 200 before tea."
                    - The Manchester Guardian, 1934.

The 1934 tour ended dramatically for Bradman. Within days of the last match and on the eve of the team's departure for Australia he fell gravely ill with a badly infected appendix and underwent emergency surgery. The cause of his long and puzzling illness was finally revealed. Jessie Bradman made a hurried trip to London to be at his side. Bradman suffered peritonitis after the operation. It was in the days before the introduction of penicillin or other powerful anti-bacterial drugs. He hovered near death for several days, but finally recovered as this happy reunion photograph in London shows.

Don and Jessie Bradman happily reunited following his brush with death.

Sir Douglas Shields, the London-based Australian surgeon who operated on Bradman and saved his life.

The Slough home of Sir Douglas, where Bradman spent some weeks recuperating after his life-saving operation in 1934.

Don and Jessie Bradman stayed in England several more weeks while Bradman slowly recuperated.
Here, they enjoy a meal together in London in December, 1934.

Bradman's friend and author, A.G. Moyes, had assisted with the hurried arrangements for Jessie Bradman to catch a train to Perth, then boat to England, and saw her off. In his book, . *Bradman*, he wrote this moving account of her departure:

"I shall never forget seeing the lonely lass starting out to cross the world, and

wondering whether her husband would be alive to welcome her. But there was a light of certainty in her eyes. She knew that she would be with her husband again.

"I was not so hopeful, and I confess without shame that I felt very sad that afternoon. These two had been sweethearts as children. They had gone hand in hand to school and then later they

had linked hands for the journey through life.

"They were so suited to one another, she in her calm, level-headed, thoughtful way acting as a brake when Don needed a bit of a jolt, as all husbands do, to prevent them from becoming too assertive in their business or sporting life. Now he needed her as never before."

A happy Don and Jessie Bradman dancing in London in January, 1935,
shortly before their return to Australia.

Following his escape from death, Bradman played no cricket in 1934-1935 and was medically unfit to make the tour to South Africa at the end of that season. After a long convalescence, he stepped back onto the first-class arena with his newly adopted State, South Australia, in 1935-1936. Looking to regain his timing and touch, Bradman started the season quietly with scores of 15 and 50 against an MCC side on its way to New Zealand. These turned out to be the entrees before the banquet. In successive matches he then scored 117 v NSW, 233 v Queensland and 357 v Victoria. Bradman finished the season with 369 against Tasmania, an innings of sheer brilliance, power and accuracy. One writer said his shots that day were *"like flights of arrows in the sun"*. He hit four sixes and 46 fours. His season aggregate in nine first-class matches was 1,173 runs, at an average of 130.33. Under his leadership South Australia won the Sheffield Shield for the first time in nine years. South Australia's gain was NSW's loss in more ways than one. Without Bradman in the NSW side, crowds and therefore gate takings at the Sydney Cricket Ground fell alarmingly. Fans stayed away by their thousands.

Don and Jessie Bradman pose outside the Kensington Park home of Bradman's new employer, Harry Hodgetts, after taking up residence in Adelaide and making a belated start learning his new job as a sharebroker.

Because of the delay in leaving England, they didn't arrive in Adelaide until Anzac Day, 1935, months later than originally planned. Bradman's decision to separate his business and sporting lives were the reason for the move. He said:

•I had proved to my own satisfaction that it was too exacting for me to live cricket day and night, and I decided completely to divorce my business life from sport.•
- Farewell to Cricket, 1950.

One of his early matches in 1935-1936 was a second-class fixture for South Australia against Newcastle, in NSW.
The camera caught this moment in the match as Bradman, on his way out to bat, had a word with the famous Australian Rugby
League player, Wally Prigg, ground-keeper at Newcastle Sportsground where the match was played. Bradman scored 46.

Catching up with correspondence in 1936. He probably received more mail than any other cricketer
in the history of the game. At the height of his career, hundreds of letters poured in each week.

He was in brilliant form against Queensland, scoring 233 in 191 minutes. He hit a six and 28 fours. In the final match of the season he scored 369 in 233 minutes against Tasmania to break Clem Hill's record for the highest score ever made on Adelaide Oval. Earlier in the season, Hill, a former Test cricketer, paid tribute to Bradman for his influence on the young South Australian Sheffield Shield side:

"With his wonderful cricket brain he has imparted a tremendous amount of confidence to the players. Keen and enthusiastic in everything he does, Bradman carries his men with him. His enthusiasm is contagious. In all my experience I have never seen a South Australian team to be so much on their toes."

Going out to bat on Adelaide Oval for his new State, South Australia, in the Sheffield Shield match against Queensland in December, 1935. His partner is C.L. Badcock.

Clem Hill.

A 1936 photograph of Don and Jessie Bradman, taken about the time he was appointed an Australian selector.

Bradman accepted the selector's position *"with some reservations"*. With the benefit of hindsight, he wrote in 1950:

A selector's job is interesting, sometimes exasperating, occasionally heartbreaking. For a captain to sit on a committee which leaves one of our trusted colleagues out of an Australian team, because in their collective judgment he must give way to a better player, is not a pleasant experience.

By Bradman's own assessment, 1936-1937 was a season of fluctuations. It opened with his appointment as an Australian Test selector. Soon after, he was appointed Captain of Australia for the Test series against England in Australia. Both the appointment and the series turned out to he controversial. Some critics believed Vic Richardson, who had been Captain on the recent successful South African tour, should have kept the job. Australia's loss of the first two Tests under Bradman's captaincy further fuelled the controversy. On the field, the season opened sensationally for Bradman when he scored 212 in a W. Bardsley and J.M. Gregory Testimonial match, which also saw his first tilt against Bill O'Reilly in a first-class match. Bradman came out on top, scoring 212, caught but not bowled by O'Reilly. He finished the season with a first-class aggregate of 1,552 at an average of 86.2. In the Tests he averaged 90. Australia eventually won the Test series after being two-down.

Bradman's Australian XI team for the W. Bardsley-J.M. Gregory Testimonial match.

Back Row – K. Gulliver, F. Ward, T.W. Leather, E.S. White, A.D. McGilvray, D. Tallon, H.I. Ebeling.
Front Row – R. Robinson, L.P. O'Brien, D.G. Bradman [Captain], C. L. Badcock, R. Morrisby.

In the W. Bardsley and J.M. Gregory Testimonial match, played at the Sydney Cricket Ground in October, 1936, Bradman captained an Australian XI against the victorious Australian touring side just back from South Africa. Bradman's team won by six wickets, but the highlight was a glorious, titanic duel between Bradman and Bill O'Reilly, meeting for the first time since their boyhood days in Bowral. Bradman, who was merciless with the other bowlers but cautious with O'Reilly, eventually won the tussle. At one stage during his innings of 212 in 202 minutes, Bradman was heard to remark:

•This chap is a marvellous bowler. I have never before so enjoyed a duel with any bowler. It is fight all the way.•

Driving Worthington in the match between an Australian XI and the MCC at the Sydney Cricket Ground in November, 1936. It was one of the first matches of the tour.

One of Bradman's most devastating run scoring shots was the pull shot. Here, perfectly balanced, he swings Verity to the square leg fence during the Australian XI v MCC match.

The match was historic because Bradman, who scored 63, captained an Australian side for the first time. He was officially appointed Australian Captain for the First Test against England in Brisbane a few weeks later.

Bill Brown and Jack Fingleton going out to open the batting for Australia in 1936. Their partnership was ironic. Brown's inclusion in the 1934 touring party to England at Fingleton's expense helped fuel Fingleton's long-standing dislike of Bradman. Fingleton believed Bradman had influenced the selectors. The selectors later strongly denied this and said the team had been chosen on form.

England Captain, Gubby Allen, jokingly makes sure Bradman
doesn't have a double-headed coin before they toss in the
First Test of the 1936 series, played in Brisbane.

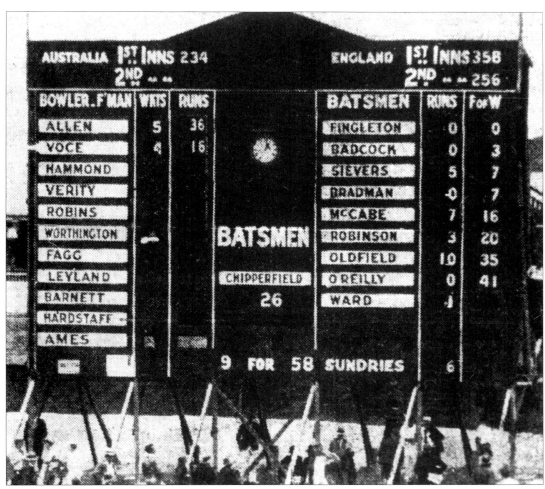

The rare sight of a scoreboard showing Bradman out for a duck.

He was caught Fagg bowled Gubby Allen for 0 in the second innings of the First Test in Brisbane, December, 1936, when England caught Australia on a "sticky" wicket after heavy rain. Australia were out for 58. It was Bradman's first Test as Captain. Australia lost by 322 runs. His captaincy in both the First and Second Tests came in for criticism and renewed calls for his replacement with the South African Tour Captain, Vic Richardson, even though Richardson's form didn't warrant his inclusion.

Vic Richardson,
Australian Test Captain to South Africa.

Rain again ruined any chance of an Australian victory in the Second Test in Sydney. England batted for the first two days and declared at 6 for 426. After heavy overnight rain, Australia was caught on their second "sticky" wicket in succession and was bowled out for 80. Bradman made his second successive duck. He scored 82 in the second innings, but Australia were all out for 324 and lost the match by an innings and 22 runs.

Right: Cutting Farnes past backward point in the second innings of the Second Test, Australia v England at the Sydney Cricket Ground, December, 1936.

Below: Playing defensively in the nets during the 1936-37 season.

Bowled Verity for 82 on the final day of the Second Test.

In the Third Test in Melbourne, it was England's turn to suffer because of the weather. The match became a battle of tactics when Bradman declared at 9 for 200 after rain turned the wicket into a *"glue pot"*. England lost wickets at such a rapid rate that Bradman, at one stage, fearing his own men might have to bat too soon on the treacherous surface, told his bowlers to stop trying to get the Englishmen out. Gubby Allen eventually woke up to that and declared at 9 for 76, but a valuable half-an-hour had been gained. In the second innings, Bradman shared a record 347 run partnership with Jack Fingleton, contributing a magnificent 270 out of a total of 564. At 18, Bradman reached 4,000 runs in all Test cricket. Australia won the match and reduced England's series lead to 2-1. Bradman believed that had Gubby Allen declared earlier, the result might have been reversed and the Ashes lost.

Bradman races to gather a shot from Hammond during the Third Test.

Batting in the nets during the 1936-1937 tour by England. The other player is Bill Brown.

Bradman has tossed but England Captain, Gubby Allen's supplication to heaven indicates the result at the start of the Fourth Test in Adelaide, 1936. Allen lost.

Bradman didn't enjoy the same reputation with the coin as he did with the bat. In Tests against England he lost more tosses than he won, although in the crucial Fourth Test of the 1936 series in Adelaide his luck changed. The toss went his way, as did the match.

Australia won the Test to square the rubber two-all. In the second innings Bradman scored a glorious 212. Many critics regarded the match-winning innings as one of the finest double centuries of his long career, even though it took more than seven hours.

Reaching his century on the first day of the Fifth Test.

After a close and fascinating series, Australia retained the Ashes with a resounding win in the Fifth and final Test in Melbourne. Bradman made 169 in Australia's only innings of 604. He is seen above reaching his century on the first day with a shot past point. Caught again on a damp wicket, England replied with 239 and 165 to lose by an innings and 200 runs.

A close call when almost run out.

Bradman lashes out at a no-ball during the Fifth Test.

During his innings, he scored his first 50 in 69 minutes, reached his century in 125 minutes and was involved in yet another record. He and Stan McCabe added 249 for the third wicket, the highest third-wicket partnership for Australia in any Test.

One of the most amusing incidents of the 1936 tour resulted from Gubby Allen's declaration at 9 for 76 during the Third Test. With bad light and rain threatening, Bradman countered Allen's declaration by sending in Bill O'Reilly and Fleetwood-Smith to open the batting and try and see out the day's play. Fleetwood-Smith could hardly hold a bat.

Bradman recalled in *Farewell to Cricket*:

I can still picture the look of incredulity on Fleetwood's face when I told him to put the pads on. He said, 'Why do you want me to open up?' and at the risk of offending his dignity I told him the truth. 'Chuck', I said, 'the only way you can get out on this wicket is to hit the ball. You can't hit it on a good one, so you have no chance on this one.' My theory was absolutely right in that not only did he fail to get out that evening, but when the game was resumed on the Monday morning, he lost his wicket to the first ball which touched his bat.

Fleetwood-Smith going out to bat. After missing every ball he faced he came off at the end of the day's play and gleefully announced that he "*had the game by the throat*".

McCabe and Bradman going out to bat during the 1936-1937 Test series.

Bradman makes his valedictory speech to an enraptured crowd gathered below the balcony of the Melbourne Cricket Ground Members' stand at the end of the Fifth Test. A disappointed English Captain, Gubby Allen, is on Bradman's right.

Bradman wrote in *Farewell to Cricket*:

Gubby Allen was most crestfallen at the loss of the Ashes, but had every reason to feel satisfied with a grand job. Injuries and illness had beset his team, and whilst I still think he could have won the Third Test match by closing his innings earlier, one must be fair and point out that rain threatened and nobody could forecast the turn of the weather which gave us a lovely wicket for the Monday.
By Test standards the batting of his team was not sufficiently reliable, but Gubby himself made amazing physical efforts to redeem any shortcomings.

The emblem on the 1936-1937 Australian blazer pocket. It was redesigned in later years.

Above: Don and Jessie Bradman at the end of the Fifth Test.

Right: Don and Jessie Bradman were a striking couple and turned heads wherever they went. This charming shot shows them looking out a train window during one of their frequent journeys around the country.

1937 - 1938

With no international matches in 1937-1938, all the Test players were available for Sheffield Shield and all vying for spots in the 1938 side to tour England. Bradman engaged in his usual run feast, averaging 98.3 in Shield matches and 81.1 in all matches, in which he batted 26 times. His highest score for the season was 246 against Queensland in Adelaide. In the return game in Brisbane, he scored two centuries in the one match, 107 and 113, the third time he'd achieved this feat in his first-class career. The season ended in further controversy with the announcement of the touring side to England. Bradman's fellow selectors took the brunt of the criticism.

Left: Bradman and his South Australian players arrive at Sydney's Central Railway station prior to their Sheffield Shield match against New South Wales in January, 1938.

Far left: Clarrie Grimmett carries his luggage along the platform.

Left: Grimmett and Bradman, ready to match skills on the tennis court.

Bradman with his fellow Australian selectors Bill Johnson and "Chappie" Dwyer in 1937.

The selectors came in for consider-able criticism soon after this photo-graph was taken for dropping veteran wicket-keeper Bert Oldfield and slow bowler Clarrie Grimmett, in particular, from the 1938 Australian side to tour England. The former Test cricketer and then member of the Tasmanian Legislative Council, the Hon. Joe Darling, said pointedly:

"Two of the three selectors have never played in first-class cricket, have never been to England and are unable to understand English conditions."

The criticism of Grimmett's absence from the side was scathing. Critics were bewildered how the selectors could ignore a bowler with 216 Test wickets to his credit, and who, although 46 years of age, was bowling as well as at any time in his career.

Clarrie Grimmett.

Bert Oldfield.

Bradman was a squash player of international standard and was ranked among the top players in Australia. In 1939 he won the South Australian amateur title in a gruelling match. He never played competition squash again because of the possible damage such intense play might do to his leg muscles.

An unusual shot with a friendly cat before a tennis match.

Playing squash against
Walter Robins in 1937.

Don and Jessie Bradman photographed in March, 1938, just prior to his departure on the 1938 England Tour, his first as Captain of the Australian side outside Australia.

1938 England Tour

As usual, the Australian side played matches in Tasmania and Western Australia before sailing to England. For the third consecutive tour Bradman opened with a double century, 258, against Worcestershire and then proceeded to score 1,000 runs before the end of May in only seven innings, thus breaking W. G. Grace's record for the lowest number of innings in performing this feat. Grace's record had stood since 1895. Australia retained the Ashes. Bradman scored 10 centuries and three double centuries. He averaged 108.5 in the Tests. In all matches he scored 2,429 runs at an astonishing average of 115.6. On the way to England the 1938 side saw the first ominous signs of a Europe preparing for a war, a conflict that was soon to engulf the world.

The 1938 Australian touring team in Tasmania en route to England. Bradman scored 79 and 144 in the match against Tasmania.

Back Row - C.L. Badcock, W.A. Brown, J. Fingleton, E. L. McCormick, W. J. O'Reilly, W. H. Jeanes [Manager], E. S. White, L. O'B. Fleetwood-Smith, F.A. Ward, C.W. Walker
Front Row - L. Hassett, A.G. Chipperfield, S.J. McCabe, D.G. Bradman [Captain], B.A. Barnett, S.G. Barnes, M.G. Waite.

The Australian cricketers caught in a serious moment during a game of bridge on board the
RMS *Maloja*. They are [left to right] W.H. Jeanes [team manager], B.A. Barnett, M.G. Waite [standing],
A.G. Chipperfield, D.G. Bradman [playing the hand] and E.S. White.

The 1938 side travelled on the RMS *Maloja* for part of the Australian leg of the tour. The team played matches in Hobart and Perth before voyaging to England on the RMS *Orontes*.

Right: The Australian cricketers also met members of the Australian women's tennis team on board the *Maloja*. Seen here [left to right] are Ben Barnett, Mrs Nell Hopman, Don Bradman and Miss Dorothy Stevenson.

One of the great characters of the 1938 side, the slow bowler Fleetwood-Smith,
seen here with Bradman on board the RMS *Orontes*.

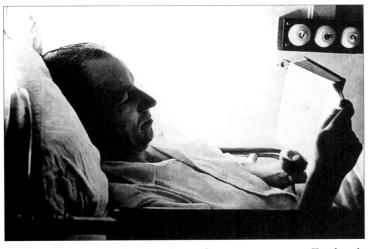

Bradman resting in his bunk on the sea voyage to England.

Fleetwood-Smith was renowned, among other things, for making strange noises on the field. Bill O'Reilly said:

"It was the oddest feeling to come in to bowl at Lord's, that sacred holy of holies, and hear Fleetwood making bird calls ."

Apart from providing a valuable rest after another tiring season, the voyage enabled Bradman to catch up on some reading and make notes which proved invaluable once the team arrived in England.

Above: This telegram boy was one of the
first to line up for Bradman's autograph
when the team arrived in England.

Right: Bradman smiles as Jack Badcock
films the team's arrival in England.

Bradman, hatless in the centre of the photograph and Lord Hawke, on Bradman's left, are almost lost among the throng of well-wishers waiting at Waterloo Station to greet the Australians on their arrival by train from Southampton in April, 1938.

At Naples on the way to England the Australian cricketers came face to face with the grim realities of nations preparing for World War II, a cataclysmic event soon to involve them all. In *Farewell to Cricket*, Bradman said they counted 36 destroyers, eight cruisers and 72 submarines.

'Marines were being drilled on the waterfront. On all sides there were obvious signs that Europe was contemplating a grim future.'

Left: Lord Hawke during his days as Captain of Yorkshire. He was also an autocratic England selector.

No matter where he went, Bradman was mobbed or followed by adoring fans, often youngsters, clutching autograph books, as shown here during a walk along Regent Street, London, with Jack Fingleton.

Fingleton wrote after the tour:

"It was embarrassing to walk down the street with Bradman, to ride in a street car or dine with him. He was instantly recognised and acclaimed. The life of the champion seemed to be one long succession of autographs. The post disgorged hundreds of letters to him daily, and almost the only peace he knew from them was while he was at the wickets - which is probably a reason why he stayed there so long.

"In all this adulation, in all this hero - worshipping, which came at its flood when he had just passed his 21st birthday, Bradman never lost his balance. He never allowed his head to expand in the vapourings of flattery.

- Brightly Fades The Don, 1949.

Right: Jack Fingleton

Flanked by members of the Australian team, Stan McCabe and Bradman share a
lighter moment before laying a wreath at the Cenotaph, London, in April, 1938.

Even on such occasions, newspaper
reporters, and individuals envious of
his success, were ever alert for things to
criticise. In Gibraltar, on the way to
England in 1938, Bradman was criticised for saluting troops with his hat off.
At the end of the 1948 tour he was
criticised for having his hands in his
pockets while walking with King George
VI at Balmoral Castle [see page 249].

In his book, *The Game Is Not The
Same*, Alan McGilvray noted:

*"Throughout his career, Bradman had
to suffer those who would seek to minimise his greatness. So many, so often,
were only too ready to carp at Don
Bradman for inconsequentials as
diverse as the clothes he wore, or the
way he spoke. The constancy of such
criticism took its toll."*

Teeing off. Peter Brough, a famous ventriloquist of the day, is to his right, leaning on a golf club.

Before the 1938 tourists settled down to serious cricket they fulfilled a number of social engagements, including a game of golf [above] and a visit to the well-known London store, Selfridge's [right], where in this publicity shot taken in April, 1938, Bradman gives store owner, Mr Gordon Selfridge, some much needed advice on how to hold a cricket bat.

In the opening tour match, Worcestershire Captain, the Hon'. C.J. Lyttleton, won the toss and paid the penalty for sending Australia in to bat on a perfect wicket. The Australians scored 541 in their first and only innings to win by an innings and 77 runs. For the third consecutive time Bradman scored a double century in the opening match of an England tour with a record-breaking 258. Bradman believed it to be the best of his three innings there.

Going out to inspect the pitch with the Captain of Worcestershire, the Hon. C.J. Lyttleton, later Lord Cobham, in the opening tour match.

In this superb action shot, Bradman is all poise, balance and power as he smashes yet another four in the opening match against Worcestershire.

The tall Victorian opening bowler, Ernie McCormick, was the centre of extraordinary scenes at the start of the Worcester match. He was no-balled 19 times in his first three overs. Bradman asked the umpire if McCormick was dragging. The reply came: *"Is he dragging over the line? He is jumping two feet over it."* Bradman, recalling the event, said McCormick shortened his run, lengthened his run, changed his pace, but still failed to rectify the trouble. At one stage he was remarking his run and got to the 19th step when a wag in the crowd called out: *"Quick, shut the gate, he'll be out on the road."* According to Bradman, McCormick never completely recovered from this early setback and only revealed his best form once or twice on tour.

Batting with Worcester Cathedral in the background.

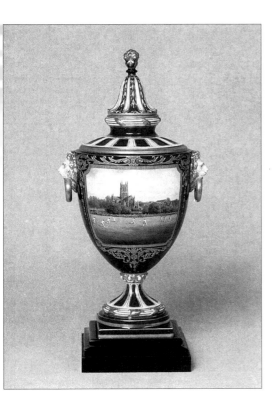

Above: The inscription on the back of the Worcester Vase, in commemoration of a "unique record".

Left: The Worcester Vase, with the cricket scene on the front.

The above photograph, from Sir Donald's private collection, is of great historical significance. It shows him batting in the opening match of the 1930 tour at Worcester with the magnificent Worcester Cathedral as a backdrop. In 1938, this scene was reproduced on the famous Royal Worcester Vase, presented to him to commemorate his third consecutive double century at the ground, a feat unequalled before or since. One of the most valuable cricket pieces in the world, the vase is in the State Library of South Australia, along with other memorabilia donated by Sir Donald.

Bradman followed his 258 against Worcestershire with 58 against Oxford University, 278 against the MCC and 143 against Surrey. A few days later against Hampshire he scored 145 not out to reach a total of 1,000 runs before the end of May, as he had done in the same match in 1930. He said later:

No other Australian had done it and as no Englishman had accomplished the feat more than once, I was keen to achieve the honour.

In the following match against Middlesex, he incurred the crowd's wrath when they thought he had terminated play by declaring the Australian innings closed 21 minutes before the end of the day. The boos turned to cheers when they realised he had done it to give Middlesex and England Test batsman, Bill Edrich, his chance to complete his 1,000 runs by the end of May. Wild cheering accompanied every one of the 10 runs needed to reach the target. In making the magnanimous closure, Bradman had been mindful of the sporting gesture in 1930 by Hampshire's captain, who could have called play off in rain and bad light, but didn't when Bradman was just a handful of runs short of his 1,000 runs.

An Oxford University bowler feels the full force of a Bradman hook.

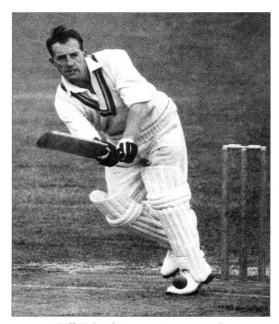

Bill Edrich in scoring mood.

Edrich and Denis Compton going out to bat in 1947. Compton made a century on debut against Bradman's 1938 side.

Captains Walter Hammond and Bradman going out to toss
in the first Test at Nottingham in June 1938.

In the First Test, England Captain, Walter Hammond, won the toss and batted on a perfect wicket. England amassed 658 for 8. With only two and a half days remaining in the match, Australia had little option but to play, successfully, for a draw. Australia's effort was marked by three superb performances. In the second innings, Bradman [144 not out] and Bill Brown [133] showed ruthless concentration in batting through most of the day to achieve the draw. However, both were overshadowed by Stan McCabe who got Australia out of trouble in the first innings with a superlative batting exhibition, scoring 232 out of a total of 411. English writer, Neville Cardus, described it as *"a great and noble innings"*. Bradman was spellbound by McCabe's batting. At one stage he called to players in the Australian dressing room: *"Come and watch this. You'll never see anything like it again."* He later said it was the greatest innings he'd ever seen, and wrote:

•Towards the end I could scarcely watch the play. My eyes were filled as I drank in the glory of his shots.•

Walter Hammond and Bradman going out to inspect the pitch before the start of the Second Test at Lord's in June, 1938.
Bradman lost the toss, as he did in all four Tests played in 1938. There was no toss in the Third Test at Manchester, which was washed out. Bradman commented dryly:

That at least saved me the indignity of losing all five on the tour.

Bradman leads his men onto the field for the Second Test at Lord's.

After England made 494 in the first innings, of the Second Test at Lord's, the London *Daily Sketch* trumpeted: "WE CAN'T LOSE NOW." They didn't but Australia ensured a draw by replying with 422, due mainly to a mammoth effort by Bill Brown, who batted right through the Australian innings for 206 not out. Bradman praised Brown, saying:

•We would have been in a sorry plight without him.•

An interesting sidelight of the Test was that the Australian cricketers were again part of world technological history. In 1930 they were among the first to talk on the new radio-telephone link to Australia. In 1938 they viewed the world's first-ever telecast of the Wimbledon tennis tournament, which was on at the same time as the Test. The players watched the tennis on a special television set provided in their dressing room.

Bill Brown.

The Second Test umpires confer with Hammond and Bradman about spectators spilling onto the field of play. On some sections of the ground there was no fence to contain spectators, who were allowed to sit on the grass right up to the edge of the boundary.

Hammond was batting at the time the umpires conferred. The disruption obviously didn't upset his concentration, because he scored 240, the outstanding performance of the Test. Bradman said of the innings:

"I have always held the greatest admiration for Hammond's cricket, but can recall no instance when his superb artistry shone so brilliantly."
    - Farewell to Cricket, 1950.

Below: A rare photograph of Walter Hammond.

Bradman takes a painful hit on the hand from England bowler Farnes in the Second Test.

Bradman scored 18 and 102 not out in the match. In the second innings he passed J.B. Hobbs' record 3,632 runs for Tests between England and Australia. Hobbs batted 71 times, Bradman only 44.

Left: A very early photograph of Jack Hobbs [left] and Archie MacLaren opening the innings for England on the second day of the 1909 Edgbaston Test against Australia. Early in his career, Bradman was inevitable measured against Hobbs and Australia's Victor Trumper, regarded as two of the greatest batsmen of their eras.

With the Third Test abandoned because of rain, Australia needed to win the Fourth Test to retain the Ashes, and did, but only after one of the most absorbing and exciting Tests ever played. It was so tense in Australia's second innings that Bradman, and others in the Australian dressing room, couldn't bear to watch. England had been dismissed first for 223. Bill O'Reilly put in an amazing performance. At one stage, his figures read 14 overs 11 maidens one wicket for four runs, two of which came from "no-balls". During Australia's first innings the light became so bad Bradman remembers matches lit in the pavilion *'shone like beacons'*, but he ordered his batsmen not to appeal against the light, fearing the possibility of rain. Australia scored 242, a lead of 19, but then dismissed England for 123, leaving Australia only 105 for victory. It looked all over until the Australian wickets began to tumble and rain clouds built up. Fearing a storm, Bradman ordered his men to force the pace. Australia lost 5 for 107 before the match was won. In *Farewell to Cricket* Bradman recalled the tense scenes in the dressing room as Lindsay Hassett saved the day:

'The match became so exciting that for the only time in my life I could not bear to watch the play. The scene in our dressing room could hardly be imagined. O'Reilly, with pads on, hoping and praying he would not be needed, was walking up and down on one side of the centre table. On the other side I was doing the same, but, to prevent my teeth chattering in excitement, was consuming copious supplies of bread and jam augmented by a liberal quantity of tea. We relied upon our colleagues to give us a running commentary of the play. This was the sort of cricket that made the spectator's blood course through his veins. In that electric atmosphere, it was Hassett who forced the issue. The imperturbable Victorian midget, who in a crisis has always been such a masterful player, lofted his drives and threw caution to the winds in a race to beat the weather. A glorious victory was achieved and we could no longer lose the rubber.'

Lindsay Hassett sweeps in a later match in England..

Bill O'Reilly: amazing figures.

This sharp Bradman return almost ended Len Hutton's mammoth innings in the Fifth Test at The Oval in August, 1938, in which he scored 364 to break Bradman's world Test record 334.

Bradman was the first to congratulate Hutton on his new world record.
Joining in is Hutton's partner, Hardstaff.

Fittingly, Bradman, fielding at short leg, was the first to congratulate Hutton on breaking his record. The match reversed the Fourth Test result and ended in what Bradman described as a *"humiliating defeat"* for Australia, losing by an innings and 579 runs. It also turned out to be Bradman's last match on the tour, an unfortunate end caused when he fractured an ankle-bone while bowling.

Bradman on the ground after hurting his ankle bowling.

As in 1934, Don Bradman's 1938 tour ended in dramatic circumstances. Australia had been forced to omit fast bowler Ernie McCormick due to neuritis in the shoulder leaving Australia insufficient firepower to break through on a feather-bed wicket. England piled on the runs. When the score had reached 887 for 7, Bradman brought himself on to relieve his exhausted bowlers, only to turn his ankle in a hole in the pitch. Later X-rays revealed a bone fracture. The photograph shows anxious Australian players gathered around Bradman, who is sitting on the pitch. The England Captain, Walter Hammond, finally declared at 903 for 7 at tea on the third day when it was clear Bradman's injury would prevent him batting in the match, an indication of Hammond's respect for Bradman's genius in winning matches. Without Bradman, Australia struggled to be dismissed for 201 and 123, losing by an innings and 579 runs, allowing England to draw the rubber, although Australia had already retained the Ashes.

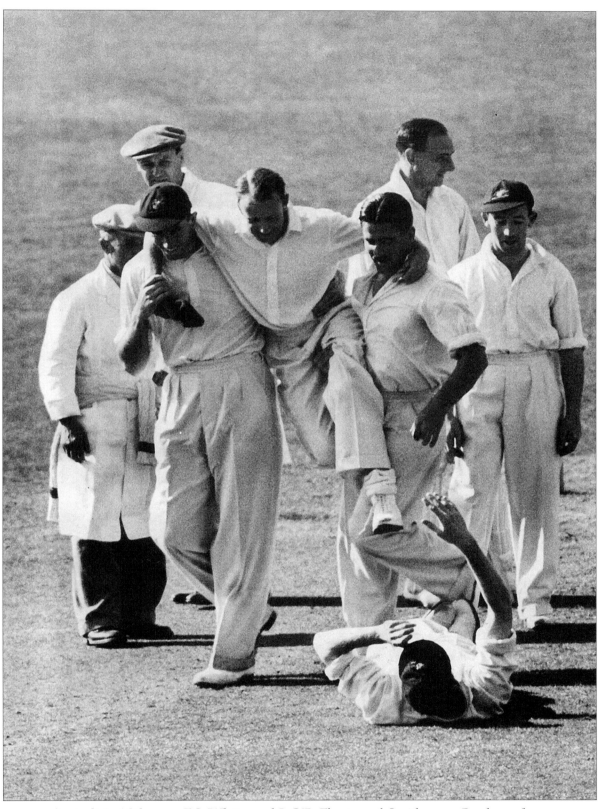

Australia's 12th man, E.S. White, and L.O'B. Fleetwood-Smith carry Bradman from the field. Bill O'Reilly is waving ruefully to Bradman from the ground, probably feeling after having bowled 85 overs and with an opposition score approaching 900, he was the one who should have been carried off.

A charming photograph of a relaxed Don and Jessie Bradman reunited in London in September, 1938, right at the end of the 1938 tour when a number of players' wives joined their husbands in England. When this photograph was taken, Bradman was still convalescing with the serious ankle injury sustained in the Fifth Test.

This rare photograph taken the same week in September, 1938, as the photograph on the previous page shows [left to right] Mrs Stan McCabe, Mrs Don Bradman, A.G. Chipperfield, Mrs W. H. Jeanes [wife of the tour Manager], Don Bradman and Mrs L. O'B. Fleetwood-Smith, enjoying tea at their London Hotel.

The presence of the wives in England had been the subject of a bitter confrontation earlier in the tour when the Board of Control in Australia refused Bradman's request that Mrs Bradman be allowed to join him at the end of the tour, the same concession extended to his predecessor, Bill Woodfull, in 1934. In banning Mrs Bradman, the Board claimed it would prevent an *"embarrassing precedent"* even though they had already done this in Woodfull's case. Bradman was infuriated, but accepted the decision. The rest of the team revolted and cabled the Board asking the decision be reversed. The Board finally relented and gave permission for all wives to join their husbands if they wished.

Bradman convalesced for some weeks at the home of former England Captain and close friend, Walter Robins. Here, left to right, Mrs Robins, Bradman, Jessie Bradman and Walter Robins rest after a walk.

Don and Jessie Bradman enjoy the gardens at the Robins' home. Mrs Robins is on the right, inspecting a plant.

1938 - 1939

Bradman, now aged 30, had hardly returned home from England when he launched into the 1938-1939 domestic season. It proved to be one of the most successful of his career. In his first six first-class innings he scored 118, 143, 225, 107, 186 and 135 not out, to equal C.B. Fry's 1901 record of six consecutive first-class centuries. Great interest centred on whether he could break the record in his seventh visit to the crease, against Victoria. However, he was out for five to a sizzling, and unlikely, catch by Fleetwood-Smith, who was never renowned for his fielding. South Australia won the Sheffield Shield under Bradman for the second time and in the winter of 1939, Bradman won the South Australian Amateur Squash Championship. In 1938-1939 he became conscious for the first time of a *"definite slowing in muscle reaction and privately was contemplating retirement from cricket".* Thankfully for cricket lovers then, and later, he decided to play on for another season.

By 1938-1939 Bradman was at the plateau of his career in terms of maturity and style, as shown by his six successive centuries in the season. But he was always quick to pay tribute to anyone who outshone him. In the opening Sheffield Shield match against NSW he scored 143, but said his innings was completely overshadowed by a *"wonderful knock"* of 271 not out by Jack Badcock.

Putting on the pads.

July 10, 1939, brought great joy to Don and Jessie Bradman with the birth of their son, John Russell Bradman. This engaging shot was taken when John was approaching the walking stage.

Right: A delightful informal shot of Jessie Bradman and son John.

Bradman's favourite portrait of his wife.
It was taken in the flower garden at their Adelaide home.

The outbreak of World War II in September, 1939, cast a bleak shadow over Australia, but it was decided to continue the Sheffield Shield competition that season because of cricket's value to national morale. Bradman ended the 1939-1940 season with 1,475 first-class runs at an average of 122.7. He rated his innings of 251 not out and 90 not out against NSW in Adelaide as probably his best ever Shield performance because he made the runs when Bill O'Reilly was at his devastating best. With events worsening in Europe by early 1940, first-class cricket virtually came to a halt and Bradman, like so many others, enlisted. He first joined the RAAF but because of delays in aircrew training he transferred to the Army, who considered they could make more immediate use of his talents, as a physical training supervisor. However, he suffered increasingly severe muscle spasms. By June, 1941, when he was invalided out of the Army, he was in constant, searing pain. In an attempt to regain his health he returned to the peaceful countryside of hometown Bowral to begin a long, trying convalescence. He then returned to Adelaide. The thought of ever playing cricket again was far from his mind. An added pressure came in 1945 with the overnight bankruptcy of his employer, Harry Hodgetts, which resulted in Bradman starting his own sharebroking business.

Right: Lieutenant Bradman at the Army's School of Physical and Recreational Training at Frankston, Victoria, in 1940. He was being trained for a supervisory role in South Australia prior to an anticipated overseas posting to the Middle East.

Below: Ready for a PT session at the Frankston Training School. Others are [left to right] Captain Beddome, Major W.J. Dickens, who was commanding officer, Sir Frank Beaurepaire and Captain "Slip" Carr.

Lieutenant Bradman and fellow Test cricketer, Sergeant Major
L.O'B. Fleetwood Smith, at Frankston Training School in 1940.

A PT squad at Frankston. Bradman is standing third from the right.

Breasting the tape in a friendly "match" race at Frankston with Sergeant-Major Max Carpenter, the famous Australian rugby international. Carpenter was touring in England when World War II broke out.

In his Army uniform while a guest with family friends at Winton, Mt Eliza, Victoria in 1941.

Max Carpenter [left] and Bradman were also friendly rivals, and occasionally allies, on the tennis court. They are seen here in April, 1941, with Australia's most famous tennis couple and long-time friends, Davis Cup players Harry and Nell Hopman.

Making a big hit with a group of Mallee girls on holiday in Melbourne in January, 1946. He had a cup of tea with them at Spencer Street railway station soon after his arrival by train from Adelaide. Note the little girl's hero-worship. The hat was borrowed for the photograph.

1946 - 1947

By the end of 1945, Bradman hadn't picked up a cricket bat in nearly five years. Much of the intervening time had been spent in an extraordinary and courageous battle against fibrositis, a muscular ailment, which he was certain had resulted from over-exertion in his earlier cricketing days. He wrote later: *"Anyone who has suffered the excruciating pain of muscular ailments will under-stand how utterly immobilising it is."* At one stage he was incapable of lifting his arm to comb his own hair and Jessie Bradman, a con-stant source of encouragement, often had to shave him. *"The job of rebuilding my health was toilsome. I often despaired of the outcome,"* he wrote. In 1945-1946 he played in two matches, but shelved further decisions about his cricket future until 1946-1947 when he returned to the first-class cricket arena very much against his doctor's advice. Ultimately, he did so because he felt he had an obligation to assist in the post-war restoration of the game, which meant so much to so many Australians. In retrospect, he said the decision to play on was the most satisfying of his cricket career. Writing in *The Bradman Albums,* he said: *"The 1946-1947 season became one of destiny... Fate handsomely repaid me by decreeing that my gamble did not fail."* Plagued by doubts about both fitness and form, Bradman embarked on the first Tests on Australian soil in 10 years. Despite a shaky start he emerged tri-umphant, scoring 680 runs in the Tests against England, with a high-est score of 234 and an average of 97.1. Bradman, the nemesis of bowlers, was back.

Jessie Bradman was an interested spectator when The Don returned
to international cricket after World War II.

Bradman returned to the internation-al scene for South Australia against the MCC in the drawn match of October, 1946. Although far from well and below form, he scored 76 and 3. The journalist R.S. Whitington unkindly wrote: *"The large crowd at Adelaide Oval yesterday watched but the ghost of a great batsman - and very few ghosts come back to life."* He was to be proved wrong. One of the interested spectators was Jessie Bradman, seen here pouring a cup of tea during the match. In rather better health and form in the following game for an Australian XI against the MCC in Melbourne, Bradman scored 106, signalling that his illustrious career was far from over. The "ghost" was about to return, and cricket lovers everywhere rejoiced at the prospect of him back with bat in hand.

The First Test team, Australia v England, December, 1946

Back Row – K. Miller, E. Toshack, D. Tallon.
Centre Row – I. Johnson, A.R. Morris, R. Lindwall, C. McCool.
Front Row – K. Meuleman, A.L. Hassett, D.G. Bradman, S.G. Barnes, G. Tribe.

Despite medical advice not to play, he made himself available for the First Test against England at Brisbane's famous Wooloongabba ground in December, 1946. His principal motive was to help re-establish post-war cricket. He felt he owed it to the game, although he had no thought of playing beyond one season. He was selected, but had misgivings about his ability to do the team justice.

J.T. Ikin, fielding at second slip, takes his controversial "catch" that wasn't.

Australia won the First Test by an innings and 332 runs, although in sensational circumstances, including a controversy involving Bradman's innings, later to become known as the *"Ikin incident"*. After a shaky start, Bradman batted with much of his old authority, eventually scoring 187. At 160 he became the first batsman in Australia v England Tests to score 4,000 runs. When 28 he attempted to guide a ball from his old antagonist, Bill Voce, through the slips cordon. It touched the bottom of his bat, then hit the ground and ricocheted to J.T. Ikin,

pictured here taking the ball waist-high at second slip. The appeal for a catch was turned down. Bradman said it was a "bump ball" and both umpires were adamant it wasn't a catch. Some English players were equally adamant it was. The controversy raged for days and lingered for years. The real importance of the incident was that had the struggling Bradman been given out at 28 and not gone on to make 187, some, including his close friend, A.G. Moyes, believed he may well have reconsidered his comeback to first-class cricket. The controversial incident seemed to settle

Bradman down. Neville Cardus wrote that after a plethora of streaky, mistimed strokes a miracle happened: *"Bradman's innings rose from the dead, a Lazarus innings."* Australia, batting first, scored what turned out to be an unbeatable 645 runs in their first innings. England had no chance when caught on two "sticky" wickets, the first after a thunderstorm and the second following a cyclonic deluge in which hailstones peppered the ground. At one point there was so much water on the ground the stumps, left lying on the pitch, floated away.

Applauding a slips catch by McCool off Miller in the Brisbane Test.

The ABC commentator Alan McGilvray was another who believed Bradman may have *"called it quits"* had the Ikin decision gone against him. He said Bradman was still not well and was under considerable strain following his return to captaincy at that late stage of his career. In his book *The Game Is Not The Same*, McGilvray said there was no doubt in his mind that Bradman was not out:

"I was broadcasting at the time and I had not the slightest doubt it was a bump ball. Lindsay Hassett, at the other end, couldn't work out what the fuss was about. He saw it as I saw it. But the Englishmen saw it differently. Even years later Ikin was adamant it was a catch. Umpire George Borwick was equally adamant it was not. So was his square leg umpire, Jack Scott."

How could he refuse? Seconds after this photograph was taken, a smiling Bradman, heading for the practice nets during the Brisbane Test, gave this young fan his autograph.

Throughout his career Bradman enjoyed considerable success with his slow spin bowling. In one match, a second-class fixture against a side in Victoria, Canada, during the 1932 tour of the USA and Canada, he had the unusual experience of taking six wickets in one eight-ball over without getting a hat-trick.

The Australian Captain bowling at the Sydney Cricket Ground nets during the Second Test against England in December, 1946.

Sid Barnes and Bradman off to the
SCG nets during the Second Test in
Sydney, in 1946.

Bradman and Hammond share a
meal during the 1946-1947 tour.
While cordial off the field, they were
fierce rivals on the field. Bradman was
criticised in some quarters for being
too ruthless in his quest for victory
over Hammond's side.

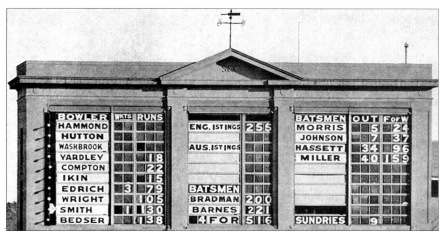

BOWLER	WKTS	RUNS							BATSMEN	OUT	F or W
HAMMOND				ENG. 1ST INGS		255			MORRIS	5	24
HUTTON									JOHNSON	7	37
WASHBROOK				AUS. 1ST INGS					HASSETT	34	96
YARDLEY		118							MILLER	40	159
COMPTON		22									
IKIN		115									
EDRICH	3	79		BATSMEN							
WRIGHT		105		BRADMAN		200					
SMITH	1	130		BARNES		221					
BEDSER		138		4 FOR		516			SUNDRIES		9

Above: The SCG scorebord showing double centuries to Bradman and Barnes. Both were out for 234.

Below: Barnes and Bradman leave the field at tea during their world record partnership in the Second Test.

The Bradman-Barnes partnership in the Second Test was one of the most memorable in cricket history, and set a world record of 405 for the fifth wicket. Bradman was out first for 234. Barnes was out soon after for the same score. He later wrote he got out on purpose [see Memories of Bradman, page 294]. Australia declared at 8 for 659 and then dismissed England twice to win by an innings and 33 runs. Bradman's effort, his fourth successive century against England in Australia [two scored before the war], was even more noteworthy because he was suffering gastritis and a leg injury when he went to the wicket. His left leg was so heavily strapped he had to play almost the entire innings off the back foot. He wrote:

•*I scarcely made one forward shot the whole day.*•

Bradman beaten in flight by England slow bowler, Doug Wright, during the Second Test at the
Sydney Cricket Ground in 1946, but his toe behind the crease foiled the
attempted stumping by Godfrey Evans.

Pulling to leg off Wright, but the ball went straight to Alec Bedser.

The Pied Piper of cricket, Bradman was surrounded by children wherever he went.
He is seen here besieged by autograph hunters during the Second Test against England at the SCG.

Ray Lindwall.

Ernie Toshack.

The former Australian Test bowler, Ernie Toshack, recalls that when NSW went over to play South Australia just after World War II, Ray Lindwall had said he'd like to "have a crack at the little fella". Toshack continued: "I said 'so would I'. But Bradman didn't play. When we saw him get his 187 in the First Test in Brisbane, Ray looked at me and I looked at him. Ray said: 'I'm pleased now that I didn't have to bowl against him', and I said: 'Yes, if we had, neither of us might be in this Test'."

Padding up during the 1946-1947 season.

England bowler, Doug Wright, unsuccessfully appeals to Umpire Scott for an lbw decision against Bradman in the Third Test at the Melbourne Cricket Ground in January, 1947. The wicket-keeper is Godfrey Evans.

The Third Test ended in a draw, the first drawn Test in Australia for 65 years. Bradman scored 79 and 49. It was the one and only time in his Test matches at the MCG that he failed to score a century. His eight Tests there produced 1,671 runs at an average of 119.3. A draw in the Third Test meant the Ashes stayed in Australia. The Fourth Test was also drawn, while Australia won the Fifth Test, an exciting encounter, by five wickets.

1947 - 1948

Having come through the Test series against England better than anticipated, Bradman made himself available for Tests against India in 1947-1948. He later announced it would be his last season in Australia, although he deferred a decision on whether he would go on the 1948 tour of England. Australia proved too strong for India, but his farewell Test performances on home soil, and an innings in which he achieved his 100th first-class century, made it a memorable, and nostalgic, season for Bradman. In his last home Tests he scored 715 runs at an average of 178.8. More importantly, he felt he'd played his part and done his best to assist the rehabilitation of Test cricket as well as Sheffield Shield cricket in post-World War II Australia.

An Australian XI v India at the Sydney Cricket Ground, November, 1947.

Back Row – R. Saggers, S. Loxton, B. Dooland, W. Johnston, R. Rogers, M. Herbert.
Front Row – K. Miller, R. Hamence, W.A. Brown, D.G. Bradman [Captain], N. Harvey, J. Pettiford.

This was the historic match in which Bradman scored his 100th first-class century. Keith Miller was batting with him when he reached the milestone.

Another classic Bradman stroke,
forcing off the back foot in the Australian XI match against India.

Right: The Sydney Cricket Ground scoreboard in the Australian XI v India match shows Bradman on 99 as he plays the shot that brought up his 100th first-class century.

Below Right: The scoreboard a few seconds later showing Bradman 100 not out and Miller 63 not out.

Below: Keith Miller, photographed during the 1950s. Bradman paid him a special tribute for his support during the innings.

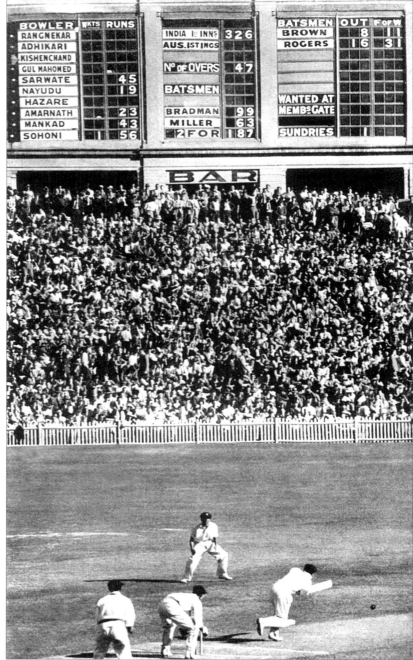

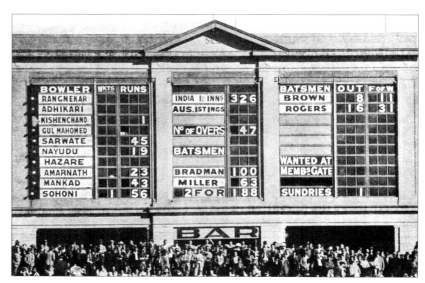

Bradman sprints down the wicket to reach his 100th century.

He went on to score 172 before throwing his wicket away. He batted for 177 minutes and hit a six and 18 fours. His partner for most of the historic innings, Keith Miller, scored 86 and gave great support. Bradman and Miller put on 252 for the third wicket, a world record against an Indian touring side. The Australian XI lost the match by 47 runs. Bradman achieved his 100th century amid amazing scenes. The atmosphere was emotional and tense as he approached the *"magic milestone"*, with the huge crowd willing him to achieve it. *In Farewell to Cricket,* Bradman wrote:

•Even in the most exciting Test match, I can never remember a more emotional crowd nor a more electric atmosphere. I think in all my experiences in cricket, that was the most exhilarating on the field. The huge crowd gave me a reception which was moving in its spontaneous warmth.•

211

John Bradman, seated on the floor fourth from the right, and some of his schoolmates
cluster around a radio in Adelaide to hear a description of how John's father,
Don Bradman, made his 100th first-class century.

He looked happy enough as he walked onto the Sydney Cricket Ground for the last time in a Test, against India in December, 1947. But it was a sad day for cricket. Over a period of nearly 20 years he had repeatedly entertained and thrilled huge SCG crowds in a way no other player had done in the history of the game. Such was Bradman's appeal that when he moved to South Australia in 1935 gate takings for Shield matches at the SCG dropped dramatically. The Indian Test proved a wet farewell. Rain ruined the match, which was drawn. Bradman scored 13 on a difficult wicket.

Below: Indian Captain L. Amarnath. Bradman regarded him as a splendid ambassador for the game and said:

'The most wonderful spirit of camaraderie existed between the Australian and Indian players.'

Bradman walks through the Members' gate onto his favourite Sydney Cricket Ground for the last time in a Test, the Second Test Australia v India in December, 1947.

Right: Walking out to bat at the Melbourne Cricket Ground during his last Test on Australian soil. After a settling-in period he was in great form and seemed set to score his fifth century of the series, but, on 57, tore a rib cartilage on the left side and was forced to retire hurt. Australia won the match by an innings and 177 runs, due in part to a magnificent 153 by a rising star of the future, Neil Harvey, playing in only his second Test. Bradman described it as an *"exhilarating"* innings.

Right: Bradman walks painfully from the field after the torn cartilage forced him to retire in the Fifth Test. Australia won four Tests. The other was drawn.

1948 England Tour

Despite concerns about his health, fitness and the possibility of failure, Bradman decided to risk one more tour of England. A great lover of England and its people, all his impulses moved him to go because he felt he had one final debt to pay to the game of cricket and its supporters, especially its English supporters who had treated him so generously and kindly during his three previous tours. Inevitably, the tour became one long, often sad, always moving personal farewell to the greatest batsman ever to grace a cricket field. Bradman himself wrote in *The Bradman Albums*:

•*It was a strange experience as I played match after match realising I would never again appear in those centres.*•

Bradman didn't disappoint, amassing 2,428 runs on tour in first-class matches at an average of 89.92 and leaving an indelible memory as he walked from the green English cricket fields for the last time. As important, he played a captain's role in a magnificent series and ended his career as the victorious leader of an Australian side he'd helped rebuild, one that became known as *"The Invincibles"* and earned the reputation as the greatest in Australian cricket history. There was relief as well as sadness. He wrote in *The Bradman Albums*:

•*There is undeniable satisfaction in having served one's country to the best of one's ability. Having achieved that I was relieved to face the prospect of returning to a life wherein the pressures of a public existence were substantially reduced.*•

Bradman [far left] with children, John and Shirley, at Parafield airport, Adelaide, where the 1948 touring side to England stopped on its way by air to Perth to join the RMS *Strathaird* for the sea voyage to London. Others in the photograph [left to right] are: Doug Ring, Neil Harvey, Ian Johnson, Bill Johnston, Lindsay Hassett, Ron Hamence and Sam Loxton.

A proud Bradman holding his children, John and Shirley,
before leaving Adelaide on the 1948 tour.
The photograph was taken at the same time as the one on the previous page.

In earnest discussion with Keith Miller about the selection of bats during a match between the 1948 Australian touring side and Western Australia in Perth, immediately prior to the tourists' departure for England by ship in March, 1948. The match was drawn. Bradman scored 115.

In his book, *Cricket Crossfire*, Keith Miller, said Bradman loved to hook, and recalled an incident during the England tour:

"I was batting with him against Yorkshire in 1948 when Ron Aspinall tried his hand at a few bumpers. Bradman hooked two in succession, smiled and walked down the pitch to my end. 'Looks as if we are going to have a bit of fun here. This fellow's going to bowl bumpers, those terrible bumpers,' he said. The Yorkshire captain deprived Bradman of his fun because he had the sense to stop the bumpers. If he had not, Bradman, in that mood, might have made a hundred in next to no time."

Two captains together, although this time captains of a different kind.
The one on the left is captain of the liner RMS *Strathaird*, Captain Allen, who has swapped hats for the photograph.

The Australian Captain introduces his 1948 side on board the RMS *Strathaird*
on the team's arrival at Tilbury, London, in April, 1948.

Others in the photograph [left to right] are Keith Miller [partly obscured behind Bradman's head], Ernie Toshack,
Ron Hamence [partly obscured], Ron Saggers, Ray Lindwall, Sam Loxton, Neil Harvey, Doug Ring and Lindsay Hassett.

Above: Two old adversaries meet again. The great England fast bowler of the 1930s, Bill Bowes, and Don Bradman shake hands on board the RMS *Strathaird* when it docked at Tilbury with the 1948 touring Australians. Bowes claimed Bradman's wicket five times in Tests and acknowledged him as the greatest batsman he'd ever bowled against.

Right: Captain, Don Bradman, and Vice-captain, Lindsay Hassett, share a joke while waiting to go ashore.

"You don't do it this way," Bradman seems to be saying to Colin
McCool during the 1948 side's first loosening-up practice session
at the Lord's nets soon after arriving in England in March, 1948.

McCool didn't play in a single Test in 1948. Many thought he had "got on the wrong side of Bradman". But in *Cricket is a Game*, published in 1961, McCool said his own poor form, not Bradman, was to blame. Bradman, he said, had always been the unfair target of vitriol both from colleagues and critics. McCool wrote:

"I liked the bloke. So far as I was concerned he was fair, just and very human. The more I remember Bradman the more I remember his warmth and understanding."

Teeing off in a charity golf game in London.

During a busy first few days at the start of the 1948 tour, Bradman played golf for the Australian cricketers in a special charity match, where [above] he set off from the first tee watched by a big audience of admirers and auto-graph-hunters. The Australians lost the foursomes 3-2 and the singles 6-4.

These occasional golfing jaunts throughout the summer are one of the cricketer's joys... It is such a relief to get away from the incessant strain - to become ordinary mortals - to be envious of some other fellow's talents, but above all to get the mental relaxation which golf so peculiarly affords.
-Farewell to Cricket, 1950.

Bradman, the Duke of Edinburgh and English Test batsman, Denis Compton, chat together at a Cricket Writers' Club reception for the Australian cricketers at Piccadilly, in April, 1948.

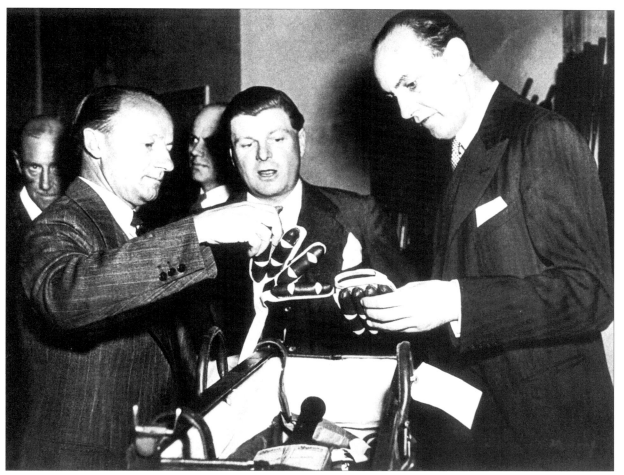

Selecting batting gloves at Slazengers in London.

The Don, as he was widely known, with Lord and Lady McGowan, at a performance of
Annie Get Your Gun at the Coliseum Theatre in March, 1948. They were among the official
guests of the management. A great music lover, he thoroughly enjoyed the night out.

From left to right: Bradman, Lindsay Hassett, Sid Barnes and Ernie Toshack, leading the group, walk out to field in the opening match against Worcestershire in April, 1948.

In all three previous tours Bradman had opened with double centuries against Worcestershire. There was enormous interest to see whether he could make it four in a row. Bradman believes he could have done so, but threw his wicket away on reaching 107, mainly because he had wanted some of his new players to get batting experience under English conditions. He followed his 107 against Worcestershire with 146 against Surrey and 187 against Essex.

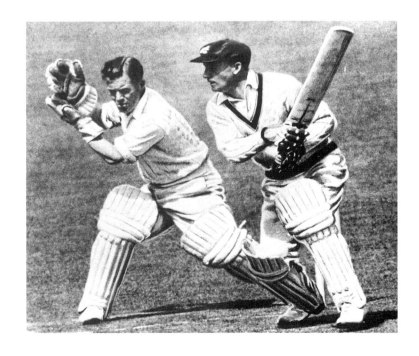

Right: On his way to a century against Worcestershire.

Attempting to catch M.R. Barton during the Surrey match at The Oval in May, 1948.

Sam Loxton.

Ron Saggers.

Australia won by an innings and 296 runs. Bradman scored 146 in 174 minutes before Alec Bedser bowled him *"with a glorious ball which pitched on the leg stump and hit the off - the same type of ball as that with which he bowled me for 0 in Adelaide in 1947"*.

In the following match against Essex, one of the lead-up games before the First Test, the Australians scored a phenomenal 721 runs in a day. They averaged 120 runs an hour. Bradman, 187, Bill Brown, 153, Sam Loxton, 120 and Ron Saggers, 104 not out, all scored centuries. Bradman's 187 was scored in 125 minutes. He twice hit 20 runs in an over. His stand with Bill Brown yielded 219 runs in 90 minutes.

Essex Captain, T.N. Pearce, and Bradman, Southend, May 17, 1948.

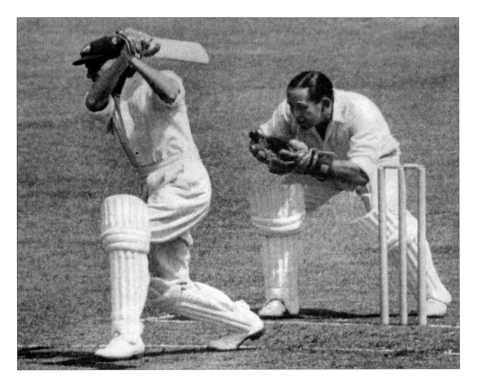

Left: Punishing Cranston with a superb off drive, against the MCC at Lord's. Griffiths is the wicketkeeper. Bradman was out caught just two short of his century.

Below: This action shot of Bradman during the 1948 tour is not one of Sir Donald's favourites because his body position is *"technically incorrect"*. While agreeing that Bradman appears off-balance, Richie Benaud believes it is an example of his marvellous footwork because it appears the ball has moved further off the pitch than anticipated, forcing The Don to change his stroke at the last second. The ball went for four.

Early in the tour Bradman was conscious of the morale-sapping effect that being no-balled 19 times in three overs had on fast bowler Ernie McCormick in 1938. He didn't want a repetition in 1948 with Ray Lindwall. Films taken in Australia showed that Lindwall's back foot was often well over the bowling crease before he delivered the ball. After consulting with the umpires at Worcester, Bradman asked Lindwall not to bowl at full pace in the match and to keep his back foot at least 12 inches behind the bowling crease to allow for the drag. The strategy worked. His deliveries were passed as fair, thereby ensuring a trouble-free tour.

England Captain, Norman Yardley, and Bradman toss in the First Test.

Leading his team onto the field at Trent Bridge, Nottingham, for the First Test in June, 1948.

Caught by Len Hutton on the leg side after glancing Alec Bedser in the First Test.

Above: Len Hutton and Bradman in 1954.

Bradman fell to the Hutton-Bedser leg "trap" in both innings of the First Test. He scored 138 in the first and was dismissed for his first ever Test "duck" in England in the second. Bradman said years later his own impatience to score runs had been the main factor in losing his wicket, because he attempted to leg-glance Bedser's in-swinger pitched at middle and leg rather than take the much safer course of simply blocking the ball.

Left: Alec Bedser, who troubled Bradman with his in-swingers.

Don Bradman's children, John and Shirley, with Jessie Bradman and their aunt,
Mrs Ray Gillam, of Sydney, in the Bradmans' Adelaide home listening to a broadcast of
the First Test of the 1948 England tour just before rain stopped play.
Australia won the Test by eight wickets.

The famous "Invincibles", the 1948 Australian touring party, photographed with the England side during the Second Test at Lord's.

Back Row–T.G. Evans [England], R.R. Lindwall, D. Ring, S. Loxton, R. Hamence, C. McCool, H.E. Dollery [England], Don Tallon.
Centre Row–R.N. Harvey, W.A. Brown, G. Emmett [England, 12th man], R. Saggers, W.A. Johnston, A.V. Bedser [England],
K.R. Miller, A. Coxon [England], E. Toshack, J.C. Laker [England], D.V.P. Wright [England], S.G. Barnes.
Front Row–D.C.S. Compton [England], I.W. Johnson, L. Hutton [England], A.L. Hassett, N.W.D. Yardley [England], D.G. Bradman,
W.J. Edrich [England], A.R. Morris, C. Washbrook [England], K.Johnson [Manager].

Left: A cut through slips in the Second Test at Lord's in June, 1948, his last Test match at this famous ground.

For the third time, he fell victim to the Bedser-Hutton leg trap in the first innings, out for 38. But in the second innings he resisted the temptation to leg-glance Bedser's in-swinger in compiling 89. Australia won by 409 runs to go two-up in the series.

Right: Signing Sykes bats at the Slazengers factory in June, 1948. He had signed thousands of Sykes bats since being contracted by the famous English bat-making firm nearly 20 years before.

Right: Signing yet more bats at Slazengers, watched by company executives.

Bradman demonstrates the classic balance and follow-through
that made his front-foot driving a legend wherever he played.

Bradman and England Captain, N.W.D. Yardley, toss at the start of the vital Third Test at Old Trafford, Manchester, July, 1948, Bradman's 50th Test. Yardley won the toss.

The rain-plagued Third Test ended in a draw, which allowed Australia to retain the Ashes. Bradman scored seven in the first innings and 30 not out in the second to help force the draw. He defended so grimly in the second innings he took 28 minutes to score his first run and batted for 122 minutes for 30 not out. As often happens, humour surfaced in the midst of crisis during the Test when Lindsay Hassett, fielding on the leg boundary, twice dropped easy catches off Cyril Washbrook from Lindwall's bowling. On dropping the second, Hassett, ever quick-witted, bor-rowed a helmet from a nearby police-man in case he should need it for a third attempt.

Bradman had an unhappy reputation for losing the toss in Tests. During the 1938 tour he called tails in all County matches with great success, but changed to heads in the Tests, believing the law of averages must operate. It didn't. He lost the toss in every Test on the 1938 tour. In 1948 he decided to call heads in all matches for the sake of consisten-cy and thinking his luck must change. Again, it didn't. He lost the toss in four of the five Tests.

Bradman was a great favourite with members of the Royal family and, in turn, he took considerable pride in his meetings with Royalty over the years, on this occasion [above] a meeting with King George VI and Queen Elizabeth during the luncheon adjournment of the match between Australia and Middlesex at Lord's in July, 1948. Australia won by ten wickets.

Left: Lindsay Hassett [left] and Don Bradman backstage at a performance of *Stars on Ice* in London, where they met skating star, Daphne Walker, whose family Hassett had stayed with in England during World War II.

Handyman Bradman uses the handle of his bat to straighten out Keith Miller's box.

Keith Miller was hit in the first innings of the Fourth Test at Leeds. The blow didn't harm Miller, who scored 58. England at that stage had the upper hand in the match, having scored 496 and taken three early Australian wickets, including Bradman's for 33. But a saviour appeared in the form of 19-year-old Neil Harvey, playing his first Test match in England. He scored 112 out of a first innings total of 458 to keep Australia in the match. In *Farewell to Cricket*, Bradman called it *"one of the greatest innings any batsman, young or old, has ever played"*. Neil Harvey and his great friend, Sam Loxton, who batted with him through most of the Leeds innings, scoring 93, were the centre of an amusing incident in the 1948 tour. In an interview for the ABC video *Cricket Archives*, Harvey recalled he'd been struggling with the

bat and, reluctant to approach the great man himself, had asked room-mate Loxton to ask Bradman's advice. Harvey recalled:

"Sam went to Bradman and said, 'My little mate wants to know what he's doing wrong.' Bradman's answer came back the same way, through Loxton: 'Tell your little mate that if he hits the ball along the ground he can't get caught'."

After Harvey's dismissal in the Test, Loxton hit what Bradman described as the *"most glorious six"* he'd ever seen. It landed 20 rows back among the crowd and was one of five Loxton hit in quick succession. One went so high that Neville Cardus wrote he got a crick in the neck watching it go.

Neil Harvey at Leeds, 1948.

Bradman and Arthur Morris, who shared one of the most amazing partnerships in the history of cricket to gain Australia an "impossible victory" in the Fourth Test [see next page].

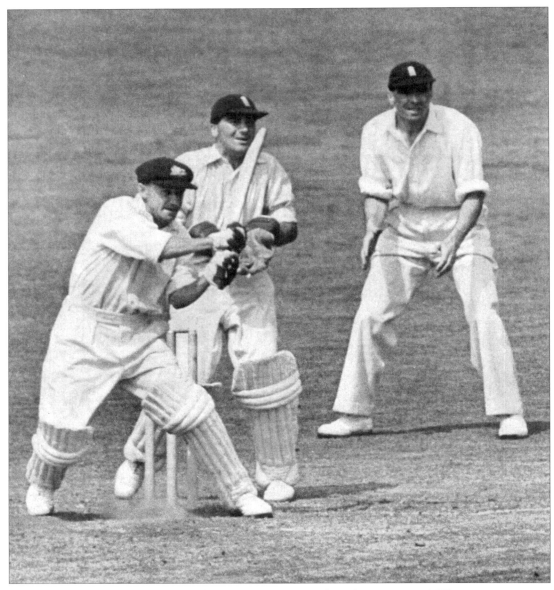

One of the many powerful strokes Bradman played in scoring 173 not out in
the Fourth Test at Leeds, a ground full of poignant memories and the scene of some of
his greatest batting triumphs. Note the combination of balance and concentration.

He received a huge ovation from the Leeds crowd at the end of the Fourth Test, in which Australia achieved what Bradman later described as a victory *"unparalleled"* in the annals of Test cricket. On the fifth and final day England had left Australia to score 404 runs in 334 minutes for victory. No previous team had ever scored more than 400 to win on the last day. Australia did with 15 minutes to spare after Bradman, 173 not out, and Arthur Morris, 182, put on 301 in 217 minutes of glorious batting. The conditions under which the runs were scored made their efforts even more meritorious. The wicket was so badly worn that some balls from Jim Laker pitched well outside the off stump but turned so far they missed the leg stump.

The ABC commentator, Alan Mc-Gilvray, who saw the match, recalled in his book *The Game Is Not The Same*, that Bradman, as a right-hander, had to stand in holes left by the bowlers. Some were two and three inches deep. He wrote:

"One on the crease was so deep Bradman's foot could not be seen from the broadcasting box. Such was the state of the pitch on which this extraordinary final day target was achieved. For sheer design, thought, purpose and utter craftsmanship, I have not seen an innings to match that one."

Again calling heads, Bradman again lost the toss in his final Test appearance, at The Oval in 1948. England decided to bat, a decision opposing Captain Norman Yardley was to rue. England were all out for 52, the lowest score ever recorded in a home Test. Lindwall took 6 for 20. Australia ultimately won by an innings and 149 runs.

A sad but memorable day as the man who had mesmerised English crowds during four tours of England leads his men onto the field in a Test for the last time, the Fifth Test at The Oval, London, in 1948.

Ray Lindwall's fluid action.

Probably the most talked-about moment in cricket history: Bradman b. Hollies for 0 in his very last innings in Test cricket.

This was the stunning exit of the world's greatest ever batsman from the Test cricket arena. Bradman, who had walked to the wicket amid a thunderous ovation lasting several minutes, was bowled second ball, misjudging a Hollies "googly". Hollies wrote later: *"I don't think Don saw it properly. He seemed to have tears in his eyes."* During his illustrious career Bradman averaged 89.77 in Tests against England. He made 11 centuries, six double centuries and twice topped 300 in Tests. With his last Test "duck",

Bradman missed out by only four runs on reaching 7,000 runs in all Tests, which would have given him a Test career average of 100.

•I dearly wanted to do well. It was not to be. That reception had stirred my emotions very deeply and made me anxious - a dangerous state of mind for any batsman to be in. I played the first ball from Hollies though not sure I really saw it. The second was a perfect length googly which deceived me.•
- Farewell to Cricket, 1950.

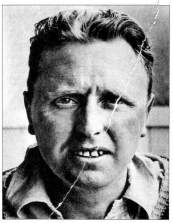

Eric Hollies

Throughout his career Bradman never made excuses for getting out. Despite the emotionally overwhelming circumstances, his dismissal for a "duck" in his final Test was treated no differently. Keith Miller was in the dressing room when Bradman returned to the pavilion. According to Miller, Bradman slowly unbuckled his pads, and simply said: *"Gee whiz, fancy doing that!"* Miller said that Bradman went up in his estimation that day and later wrote of The Don's reaction: *"It proved that Bradman was as human as any other member of the team."*

Above: The scene on the Members' stand balcony at The Oval at the end of the Fifth Test when Bradman [left front, dressed in a suit] farewelled the big crowd. Then the England Captain, Norman Yardley [in the dark jacket on the right], called for three hearty cheers for Bradman. Yardley told the crowd: *"We are saying goodbye to the greatest cricketer of all time: a great cricketer and a very great sportsman, on and off the field."*

Left: Bradman cuts the cake made specially to commemorate his last Test appearance, in the Fifth Test at The Oval, August 14 to 18, 1948. With him is the England Captain, Norman Yardley.

241

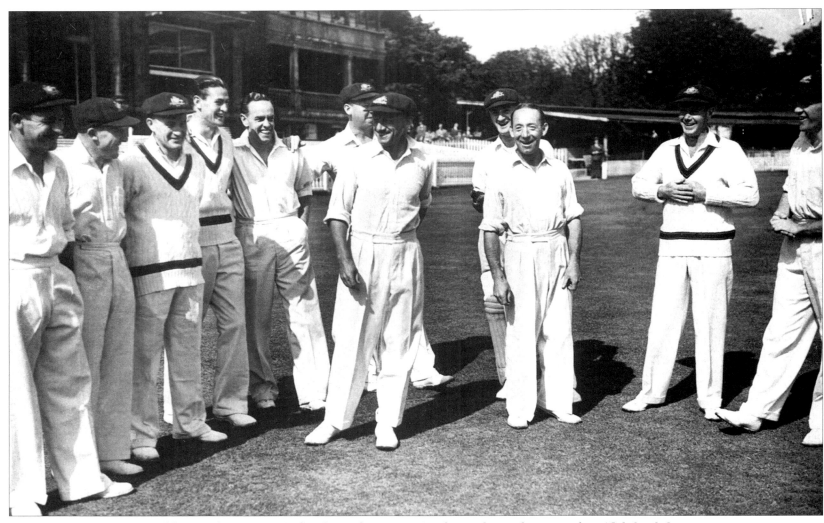

Led by Lindsay Hassett, the Australians give Bradman three cheers on his 40th birthday, which fell during the Gentlemen of England match at Lord's in August, 1948.

It was another emotional day because it was Bradman's last at the headquarters of cricket. He made up for some of his disappointment for his "duck" at The Oval by scoring a magnificent 150. Australia won by an innings and 81 runs. Bradman later wrote in *Farewell to Cricket:*

So it was on my 40th birthday I left forever the headquarters of cricket, happy in the knowledge of a great win, a century, a host of wonderful friends and an abiding conviction that I must have played the game as it should be played to earn these warm-hearted tributes. No man could have ordered his cricket life better than to end at headquarters on such a congenial note, and it was with mixed feelings of pride and sadness I drove through the Grace Gates that evening.

Vice-Captain, Lindsay Hassett, who was of great assistance to Bradman on tour and succeeded him as Captain.

Sid Barnes and Bradman coming out to resume his last first-class innings in England, at Scarborough in September, 1948.

Bradman scored 143 against the South of England and a triumphant 153 - his 11th century of the tour - against a near Test strength H.D.G. Leveson-Gower XI in his last two matches on English soil. He bowled the last over of the very last match - and had led an Australian team through an England tour undefeated.

The final tour match was against Scotland, in Aberdeen. Beforehand, the Australians played a farewell game of golf. They posed for this photograph [right] before hitting off. Bradman is in the front row on the left. Others shown include Keith Miller, Ray Lindwall, Doug Ring, Ian Johnson and Bill Brown.

In *Farewell to Cricket* he wrote of the 1948 side:

'History may decide whether it was the greatest Australian team ever, I can't. For me, I'm satisfied to say it was a really great team, whose strength lay in its all-round ability, versatility and brilliance allied to bulldog courage. You can often get some of these things; to get the lot is a rarity.'

Right: A great leader of men leads his triumphant Australian side for the last time in the last match of the tour, against Scotland in September, 1948.

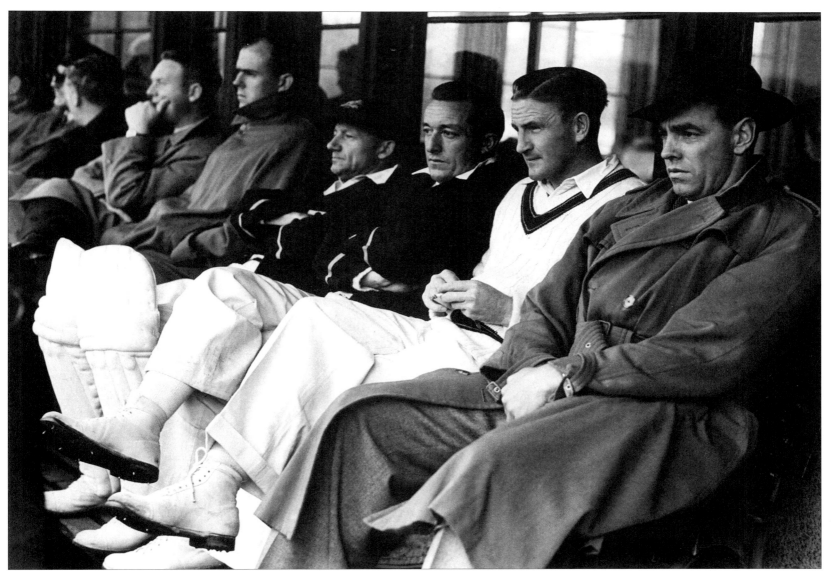

Bradman, with the pads on in the centre of the photograph, waits to bat against Scotland. Fittingly, the master batsman
finished his fourth and final tour of England and Scotland with a century, 123 not out.
Pictured [left to right] are: Doug Ring, Bill Johnston, Don Bradman, Ron Hamence, Colin McCool and Ian Johnson.

Bradman's great sense of humour emerged when he returned to the dressing room after his Scotland innings. Lindsay Hassett, stretched out on a form, looked up and said sleepily: *"What happened, did you chuck it away?"* *"Well,"* said Bradman with a wide smile, *"I worked out that to average 100 for every innings I have had in England I would have had to make about 500 not out, and this game, as you know, is limited to three days."*

Above: It was an equally nostalgic moment for Australian batsman Bill Brown [left], also playing his final match on British soil. Brown had partnered Bradman in many memorable innings since they first came together in the 1930s.

Left: Bradman doffs his cap to the applauding crowd as he walks off the field in Scotland, his last match in the British Isles.

Above: One of Bradman's treasured memories came after the Scotland match in September, 1948, when he and members of the Australian team were guests of King George VI and Queen Elizabeth at Balmoral Castle. Here, he introduces the team. The Queen is shaking hands with Colin McCool.

Left: Chatting with Queen Elizabeth and Princess Margaret.

Above: This informal photograph shows the Australian cricketers and members of the Royal family strolling across the grounds of Balmoral Castle following the Scotland match.

Left: The Duke of Edinburgh and The Don at Balmoral Castle.

Below: This much published close-up shot of King George VI and Don Bradman, taken at the same time as the wider photograph [left], brought howls of protest from the British Press because Bradman had his hands in his pockets. But as the wider shot shows, Bradman wasn't the only one. It was pointed out it was an informal occasion and a cold day.

Bradman wrote later:

•Subsequent events rather tend to indicate that at least His Majesty was not displeased.•

He was referring to the fact that the following year, King George conferred a Knighthood on Bradman, the first ever on an Australian cricketer.

During the Balmoral Castle visit, King George VI, with a twinkle in his eye, said to Australia's official scorer:

"Tell me, Mr Ferguson, do you use an adding machine when The Don comes to bat?"

A happy scene at a farewell luncheon at the Savoy Hotel, London, in September, 1948, as Bradman joins hands with distinguished British newspaper executives, H. Ainsworth [left] and A.G. Cousins, OBE [right] during a robust rendering of "Auld Lang Syne".

At the luncheon Bradman was presented with a silver replica of the famous Warwick Vase, purchased from a Shilling Fund subscribed to by cricket lovers all over the British Isles. He requested that money left over be used to lay concrete pitches in parklands throughout England to help foster cricket. He wrote:

To me this trophy will always convey a special memory of the kindness of the common folk of England, and will serve to remind me of four wonderful cricket seasons in their midst which I am delighted to think brought some pleasure and enjoyment to their lives.
        - Farewell to Cricket, 1950.

Lord Gowrie, VC, President of the MCC, presents Bradman with the Warwick Vase replica.

During the lunch Bradman shook hands with Don Clark, named Donald after the famous cricketer. Along with nine other youngsters, he represented the thousands of English fans who contributed money to the Shilling Fund used to commission the Warwick Vase replica.

Scores wrote letters, some humorous. One of the many youngsters who subscribed wrote:

"Thank goodness you've quitted. Perhaps we'll have a chance now. I'm sending my shilling in thankfulness."

Left: Signing autographs at the farewell lunch.

Bradman says goodbye to a good friend, a friendly foe and a fine cricketer,
England Captain, Norman Yardley, at the Savoy Hotel lunch.

A few days later, Yardley was among those to farewell the Australians when they sailed from Tilbury. In *Farewell to Cricket* Bradman wrote:

As I watched the pier gradually recede, the handkerchiefs waving - not all of them dry - I really felt here was the end of a mission. It had been without doubt in every sense the grandest tour of all...Whatever inspired me to go, I felt it had been ordained for a greater purpose than the pleasure or success of individuals - it had been my destiny to do what I could for cricket and in my heart I knew I could not have done more.

Home at last. Jessie Bradman and children welcome him at the end of
the exhausting, but highly satisfying, 1948 tour.

Bradman's sense of humour emerged yet again at a press conference just before leaving England when he told an amusing story about a telephone call to Jessie Bradman back in Australia. When she answered, Bradman said: "*Hello, is that you, darling?*" Jessie: "*Yes, darling, who is that?*" Bradman told the reporters that, after six months away, he thought it was about time he went home.

On his return from England Bradman had no intention of ever playing in a first-class match again, but then agreed to appear in three Testimonial matches as a final curtain call before an adoring Australian public. The first was his own Testimonial, at the Melbourne Cricket Ground. The second was the Alan Kippax-Bert Oldfield Testimonial in Sydney. His final first-class appearance was for South Australia against Victoria, a Testimonial match for long-serving South Australian and Test batsman, Arthur Richardson. The crowning achievement of his career came in January, 1949, with the announcement of his Knighthood in the New Year's Honours list, the highest honour ever bestowed on an Australian cricketer. Statistics tell the story of his astonishing career.

He batted 669 times, 338 in first-class matches and 331 in second-class matches, scoring 50,731 runs overall at an average of 90.27. In all first-class matches he scored 28,067 runs at an average of 95.1 and in Test cricket 6,996 runs at an average of 99.94. His Sheffield Shield average after 96 innings was 110.19. He scored 117 first-class centuries, including 29 in Tests.

Above: In familiar pose, signing autographs on arrival at the MCG during his Testimonial match.

Right: Talking with Arthur Richardson, the former Test batsman. Bradman's last first-class appearance was in Richardson's Testimonial match at Adelaide Oval.

More than 90,000 spectators attended Bradman's Testimonial at the MCG
in December, 1948. Here, The Don receives the adulation of fans
as he goes in to bat for D.G. Bradman's XI against A. L. Hassett's XI.

It was to be a remarkable event. To the huge crowd's delight Bradman scored 123 - his 117th first-class century - and took a wicket with the last ball he ever bowled in a first-class match. The game ended in a dramatic tie, due mainly to a magnificent innings by Don Tallon, who, playing for Bradman's team, figured in a 100-run, tenth-wicket partnership of which he scored 91, hit 12 off the last over and levelled the scores off the last ball.

Bradman played one final match at his favourite Sydney Cricket Ground, the Testimonial for Alan Kippax and Bert Oldfield in February, 1949. The teams, photographed here, were captained by Arthur Morris and Lindsay Hassett. Bradman played in the Morris XI.

Back Row–J. Moroney [M], J. Burke [H], K. Archer [M], G.A. Langley [M], W. Donaldson [12th man], P. Ridings [H].
Centre Row–H. Elphinston [Umpire], K. Meuleman [H], F. Johnston [H], K.R. Miller [H], D. Ring [M], W. Johnston [M], R.A. Saggers [H], L. Johnson [M], I. Johnson [M], G. Borwick [Umpire].
Front Row–V.N. Raymer [H], A. Walker [H], R.A. Hamence [M], R.N. Harvey [H], A.L. Hassett, A.R. Morris, D.G. Bradman [M], R.R. Lindwall [M], S. Loxton [H].

Arthur Morris leads his team onto the SCG.

It was the first time in more than 15 years that Bradman, now Sir Donald following his Knighthood in the New Year's Honours list, had played without captaining the side. Keith Miller recalled there was a delightful moment during the match when Sir Donald Bradman first arrived at the "Visitors'" dressing room. The door-attendant, "Smithy", had known Sir Donald for years and had always called him "Don", but this time there was a momentary hesitation. Before he could say anything Sir Donald said: *"It's still Don, Smithy."*

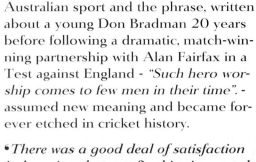

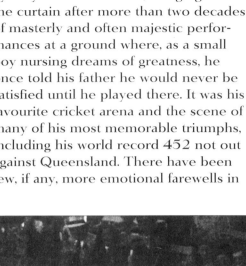

Sir Donald Bradman goes out to bat for the last time on his beloved Sydney Cricket Ground, bringing down the curtain after more than two decades of masterly and often majestic performances at a ground where, as a small boy nursing dreams of greatness, he once told his father he would never be satisfied until he played there. It was his favourite cricket arena and the scene of many of his most memorable triumphs, including his world record 452 not out against Queensland. There have been few, if any, more emotional farewells in Australian sport and the phrase, written about a young Don Bradman 20 years before following a dramatic, match-winning partnership with Alan Fairfax in a Test against England - *"Such hero worship comes to few men in their time"*. - assumed new meaning and became forever etched in cricket history.

There was a good deal of satisfaction in knowing that my final innings on the ground I loved so well contained a few strokes of the old vintage.
    - Farewell to Cricket, 1950.

Left: Walking off the SCG after his last innings there in February, 1949. He scored 53. Cricket writer, R.S. Whitington, observed:

"Sir Donald Bradman again rose grandly to the big occasion to score one of his finest fifties."

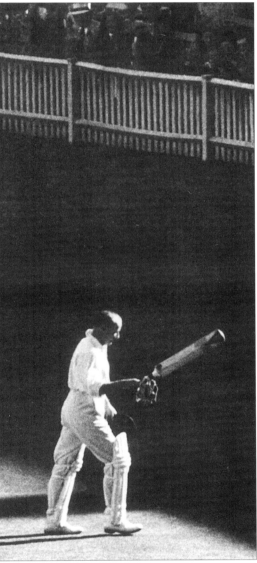

In March, 1949, Sir Donald Bradman received his Knighthood, a unique tribute which recognised his magnificent contribution to cricket and to his country. But his service to cricket was far from over. He remained in cricket administration at both State and national level for many years. In 1960 he became the first Test cricketer to be elected Chairman of the Board of Control. He was an Australian selector until 1971 and held numerous positions with the South Australian Cricket Association until his retirement from the association's most senior position, that of President, in 1975. In February, 1963, Sir Donald made his *"positively final"* appearance at the wicket, as Captain of the Prime Minister's XI v the MCC. All involved dearly wanted Sir Donald to make at least 50. But as so often happens in cricket, fate and luck intervened. After facing four balls and scoring four runs, he played defensively to Brian Statham. The ball trickled off his bat between his feet and Sir Donald accidentally kicked it onto the base of the stumps. He never faced a bowler in a match again. In 1979 he was invested with Australia's second-highest civil award, that of Companion of the Order of Australia. Now 86, Sir Donald still has an active interest in cricket both as a spectator and a significant contributor to the welfare of the game through the Bradman Museum and other organisations. Unlike some of his contemporaries, he enjoys the modern one-day game. Asked if he would like to have played it he says, almost with a glint in his eye: *"I would have loved it."*

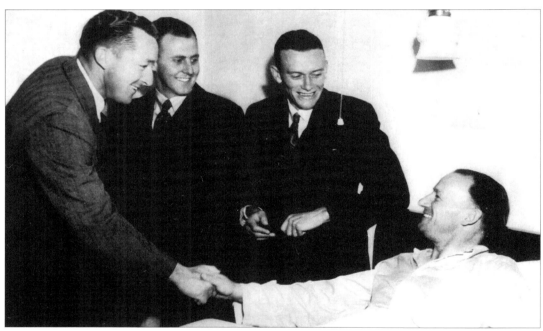

Right: Being congratulated in his hotel room on the morning his Knighthood was announced in the King's New Year's Honours List on January 1, 1949. Ron Hamence is shaking his hand. The others are Len Michael [centre], and Phil Ridings.

Right: Bradman was a favourite subject for cartoonists throughout his career. Here is how two famous artists saw him. Left to right: Berto, whose work was originally published in the *Sydney Sun,* and Tony Rafty, the famous Sydney cartoonist, who drew his caricature for a limited edition print of Sir Donald.

Sir Donald chats to Captain Vivian Bullwinkel after receiving his Knighthood from the Governor-General, Mr McKell, in Melbourne, March, 1949. Lady Bradman is on the far right.

The Melbourne *Herald* poster of March 15, 1949, the day Sir Donald was knighted.

Captain Bullwinkel was awarded the Order of the Royal Red Cross. She was the sole survivor of the Banka Island massacre during World War II in which Japanese soldiers murdered 29 nursing sisters. As explained below, Sir Donald later revealed had he thought his Knighthood was purely a personal award he would have declined it.

'When I started my Test career I had no thoughts of anything but the love of the game, the joy of playing it and the honour of representing my country. I stood in awe when informed of the King's wish and sincerely believe I would have declined the honour had there been nothing to consider but my personal feelings. However, I recognised it was intended as a compliment to the game of cricket and Australian cricket in particular. To refuse would have been ungracious. So I accepted, even though I knew that life would never be quite the same again. I must confess that I felt a sense of pride that my wife could thus share in a positive way some reflected glory and she always bore her new-found status with grace and dignity worthy of any title. But for me personally, as a private man and a citizen, I always preferred to think of myself just as plain Don Bradman, the boy from Bowral.'

- The Bradman Albums, 1987

Sir Donald and Lady Bradman in the garden of their Adelaide home after
their return from England in 1953, when Sir Donald reported the 1953
Australian cricket tour as a special writer for the London *Daily Mail*.

A family photograph of John and Shirley
Bradman taken in the early 1950s.

Sir Jack Hobbs and Sir Donald meet again during one of Sir Donald's visits to England.

This early photograph of Jack Hobbs, showing his relaxed stance, is from Sir Donald's private collection. Sir Donald is a great admirer of Hobbs' talents and rates him as one of the all-time greats.

An even earlier shot of Hobbs [right] with Herbert Sutcliffe, probably England's greatest opening pair. They are seen here with silver tea and coffee services presented to them for their magnificent centuries against Australia in Melbourne in 1924-1925. Together, the pair exceeded 100 for the first wicket 15 times.

Renewing acquaintances with Queen Elizabeth II and Prince Philip at Adelaide Oval during the Royal Visit in March,1954. He had met them previously in England.

Lady Bradman and John Bradman in London in 1956. The family accompanied Sir Donald to England where, as a newspaper correspondent, he reported on the 1956 Australia-England Test series.

John Bradman became a champion hurdler. He won a South Australian title and, up until the time a serious knee injury ended his athletics career, he was a strong contender to represent Australia at the Olympic Games. It was a remarkable and courageous achievement considering the fact that he had been stricken with polio at the age of 12 and spent eight months in a steel brace.

The Bradman family, Sir Donald, Lady Bradman, John and Shirley at home in Adelaide in May, 1956.

Right: Leaving the field after umpiring a cricket match in Adelaide. Sir Donald had been a qualified umpire since the mid-1930s.

Right: Concentrating during the match.

Sir Donald, always a top-class golfer, probably reached the pinnacle of his golfing career in the early 1950s when he reduced his handicap to scratch and became a pennant player. As in tennis, there is little doubt Sir Donald could have played golf at the highest level had he ever taken it up seriously. At 86, he is still playing regularly and still able to score less than his age, a rare feat.

Left : Lady Bradman and Shirley Bradman watch Sir Donald practising his swing before the Kooyonga Golf Club Championships in 1961.

Left: The umbrella was a necessary part of the equipment on this day in Adelaide in 1955, just before Sir Donald and H.M. Langdon set out in heavy rain in the South Australian Amateur Golf Championships at Royal Adelaide.

Right: Signing an autograph for a young admirer in February, 1963, when he played for a stockbrokers' team in a social match in Adelaide.

Below: Surrounded by more young autograph hunters as he leaves the field during the match.

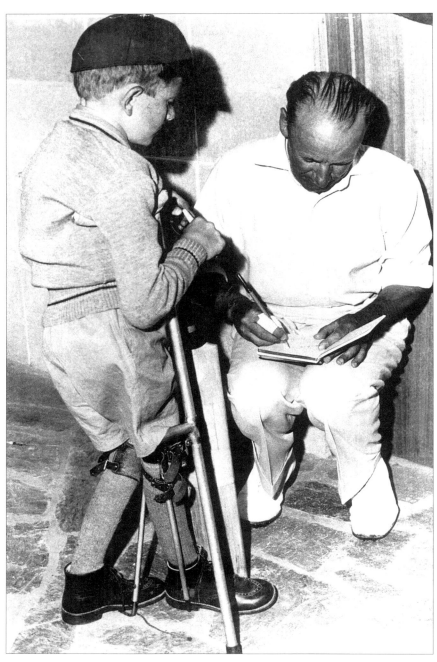

Right: Sir Donald has always had great affection for children and has been magnanimous and unstinting helping charities involving them. A touching reminder of this private and little known generosity came in the form of this birthday card, from the Goodwill Children's Village, in India, a home for underprivileged and orphaned children, which he has supported for many years. All the children signed the card [see far right].

Happy Birthday
FRIEND

True friends are mighty
hard to find --
It isn't every day
One comes along that seems to be
Just right in every way,
That's why this Happy Birthday wish
Is meant to tell you, too,
How much it means to have a friend--
A perfect friend--like you.
Happy Birthday

From everyone at
Goodwill Children's Village

Bradman walks onto a cricket field as a player for the last time, as Captain of the Prime Minister's XI v The MCC at Manuka Oval, Canberra, in February, 1963.

Richie Benaud once lamented to Keith Miller he'd missed out playing against Sir Donald by only a year. Sir Donald retired the year before Benaud came into first-class cricket. Miller replied: *"You should count that as an advantage, young man, because he would have belted you around just like he did the rest of us."*

Sir Donald's well-known sense of humour emerged in another story concerning Richie Benaud. In his final first-class season the South Australian Cricket Association farewelled Benaud at a cocktail party at Adelaide Oval. During proceedings, a cricket official referred several times to *"a household name"* and *"a name no one will ever forget"* and then promptly introduced him as Richie *"Benny"*. A few weeks later the famous American comedian, Jack Benny, arrived in Australia. Benaud turned up at a Test match to find a note in Sir Donald's handwriting with a press clipping about Benny pinned to the Australian dressing room door . The note said: *"Your brother, I presume."*

Sir Donald Bradman and Richie Benaud in 1964.

Four famous Test captains, Sir Donald Bradman, Richie Benaud, Bill Lawry and The Nawab of Pataudi, sign a cricket bat during a reception in Sydney in February, 1968, for the visiting Indian cricket team.

Les Favell, Rex Sellers, Neil Hawke, Barry Jarman and Sir Donald with the Sheffield Shield in a winning year for South Australia.

Demonstrating a point about footwork and balance to Australian opening batsman and later Captain of Australia, Bob Simpson.

The world's greatest batsman and the man Sir Donald regarded as the world's greatest bowler, Bill "Tiger" O'Reilly, together again at the official re-opening of Bradman Oval, Bowral, after upgrading work in 1976. The oval is the same site where they first met as cricket antagonists more than 50 years earlier. They are seen here [left] walking off the field after O'Reilly had bowled one last ball to Sir Donald. The ball went down the leg side. Sir Donald's attempted hook missed [see below].

Above: Sir Donald swings and misses as the ball from Bill O'Reilly goes well down the leg side. This was Sir Donald's last appearance on a cricket pitch.

Above: A sign erected at Glebe Park after it was re-named Bradman Oval in 1947.

O'Reilly and Bradman walk from a cricket field together for the last time, at Bowral in 1976.

273

Sir Donald Bradman met some of his old England foes from the 30s and 40s at this nostalgic Anglo-American
Sporting Club Dinner held in his honour in London in May, 1974. Shown are:
Back Row - [left to right], D.V.P. Wright, D.C.S. Compton, R.T. Simpson, A.V. Bedser, J.C. Laker and J.G. Dewes.
Front row - R.W. J. Edrich, N.W.D. Yardley, Sir Donald Bradman, Sir Leonard Hutton and T.G. Evans.

Between them the three men photographed right, Sir Donald Bradman, Sir Leonard Hutton and Sir Garfield Sobers, reached extraordinary cricketing heights. Sir Leonard scored his world Test record 364 against Bradman's 1938 touring side, breaking Sir Donald's previous world record 334. In turn, Sir Garfield broke Hutton's record with 365 not out against Pakistan in Kingston in 1958. In 1973, Sir Garfield gave what Sir Donald, perhaps modestly, described as *"probably the greatest exhibition of batting seen in Australia"*, his 254 runs in 376 minutes for the Rest of the World against Australia.

Three cricketing Knights, Sir Leonard Hutton,
Sir Garfield Sobers and Sir Donald Bradman
at a centenary dinner in Adelaide in 1984.

Dennis Lillee, Sir Donald Bradman and Harold Larwood.

Sir Donald shares a private moment with two of cricket's greatest fast bowlers, his great adversary of the 1930s, Harold Larwood and latter-day Test player, Dennis Lillee. They were attending the Centenary Test at the Melbourne Cricket Ground in March, 1977, which captured the imagination of cricket lovers and brought together the greatest names in the game. In an extraordinary repeat of history, Australia won the Centenary Test by 45 runs, the same result as the first Test played between the two teams in 1877.

ABC commentator, Norman May, [below] often tells the story about the interviewer who asked Sir Donald what he thought he might have averaged against a West Indies fast bowling attack. Sir Donald, renowned for his dry sense of humour, pondered a while and replied: *"44.44."* Knowing that Sir Donald's Test average was 99.94, the somewhat incredulous interviewer said: *"Only 44.44."* Sir Donald: *"Yes, after all, I am 85."*

Norman May.

Alan Davidson.

Sir Donald's sense of humour again surfaced during the famous tied Test between Australia and the West Indies in Brisbane in 1960-1961. Alan Davidson recalled: *"I broke the little finger on my bowling hand during catching practice before the game even started. Only Sir Donald, Richie Benaud, the Captain, and I knew about it. I finished having an amazing match. I took 11 wickets and scored 124 runs to set a new world record by taking more than 10 wickets and scoring more than 100 runs in a Test. In the excitement about the tie, my world record was largely forgotten, except by Sir Donald, who came up and said: "Pity you didn't break your finger before the other Tests'."*

Members of the famous Australian 1948 side at a reunion hosted by
the Governor of NSW, Sir Roden Cutler, VC, at Government House, Sydney, in 1979.

Back Row – Neil Harvey, Ray Lindwall, Ron Saggers, Doug Ring, Bill Johnston, Ernie Toshack, Keith Miller, Don Tallon, Sam Loxton.
Front Row – Ron Hamence, Ian Johnson, Lindsay Hassett, Sir Donald Bradman, Bill Brown, Arthur Morris.

Fifteen of the 17 players in the touring party attended the reunion.
The other two tourists were Sid Barnes and Colin McCool.

The short and the tall. The Governor of NSW, Sir Roden Cutler, VC,
and Sir Donald Bradman enjoy a joke at the 1948 team reunion at Government House,
Sydney, in 1979. Sir Roden is now Patron of the Bradman Museum.

Above: Sir Donald with West Indies Captain, Clive Lloyd, and team Manager, Esmond Kentish, when they presented him with a book on the life of the legendary West Indian cricketer, George Headley.

Above right: The only photograph ever taken of Sir Donald and the great West Indies batsman, Viv Richards, together. They were in the dressing room at Adelaide Oval. Sir Donald rated Richards very highly as a batsman.

Right: This photograph of Lady Bradman and Sir Donald, dining in Melbourne, is historic for two reasons. It was taken at a dinner during the opening of the Australian Sporting Hall of Fame. Sir Donald was the No 1 inductee. It is also historic because it was one of the few photographs taken of Sir Donald wearing a moustache, which he kept for only a short period of time.

Sir Donald made a rare public appearance in his Australian blazer and a green baggy cap during a Testimonial match in Adelaide in 1987 for close friend and veteran Australian and South Australian batsman, Les Favell, seen here alongside Bradman at the match. The former Test left-hander, Neil Harvey, is on Favell's right.
Bradman had to borrow the cap having given all his own away during his career.

Above: With the great Bill Ponsford at a luncheon in Melbourne, 1985. Bradman and Ponsford shared many memorable batting partnerships.

Left: Guest of honour, Les Favell, and Sir Donald, acknowledging the crowd, walk onto Adelaide Oval.

Sir Donald Bradman and one of his closest cricketing friends, the former England Test batsman, Denis Compton, share a joke at a London dinner, given in Sir Donald's honour in 1974.

Sir Donald and Sir Colin Cowdrey take block for the cameras during a visit to Adelaide Oval.

This happy occasion marked Sir Donald's 85th birthday in 1993. Denis Compton, centre, flew specially from London for the birthday dinner with Sir Donald and Lady Bradman.

Left: Sir Donald and Lady Bradman made a rare public appearance in Bowral, for the opening of the Bradman Museum on Saturday, October 14, 1989. Lady Bradman is seen here officially unveiling the plaque.

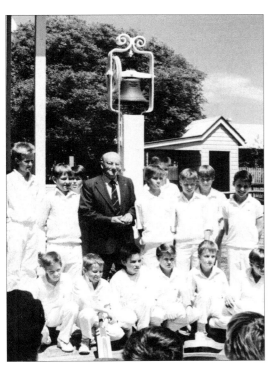

Far Left: While in Bowral, Sir Donald visited Bowral Primary School where he was photographed beside the bell post which served as a wicket for playground matches when he was a pupil there.

Left: Sir Donald's youngest sister, May, his only surviving brother or sister. She still lives in the Bowral district.

A charming candid shot of Sir Donald and Lady Bradman, sharing a lighter moment at the opening of the Bradman Museum, Bowral, in 1989. Childhood sweethearts who later married, they have enjoyed a deep and abiding lifelong relationship, which Sir Donald has often called the *"greatest partnership of my life"*.

"The word Bradman... has become synonymous with more than mere excellence. There is a ring to it of excellence of an order that will never be equalled again.
"The Bradman Museum will have 100 autographed bats one of which will be presented annually to the player of the year. When all the bats are given away, it is safe to say that Sir Donald's records and legend will remain unchallenged."

- The Sydney Morning Herald, Saturday, October 14, 1989, the day of the Bradman Museum opening.

Below: Sir Donald, with Lady Bradman at his side, waves to the crowd at the Bradman Museum opening.

"Despite all the decades of publicity, of hero-worship, he remains a sincere, unassuming and kindly man, just as Lady Bradman remains a serene and charming woman. Her influence on this remarkable partnership, which has already lasted more than half a century, cannot be overestimated. In some miraculous way they have retained all the homely virtues of their upbringing in a little town in the 'old' Australia. Don Bradman is forever a part of the history of Australia and as with most historic figures there is a certain mystery about him which cannot be solved. There are no words to define genius. Don Bradman was the genius of the cricket pitch, and we shall not look upon his like again."
–Michael Page, in his 1983 biography, Bradman.

The Bradman Museum

The Bradman Foundation was formed in 1987, its main aim being to establish, through the Bradman Trust and Museum, a living cricket centre commemorating Sir Donald Bradman AC.

The Museum is located adjacent to Bradman Oval, in the open parkland setting of Glebe Park, Bowral, where Sir Donald's cricketing career began. Cricket has been played on the ground since the 1890s and in 1947 it became known as Bradman Oval. Don Bradman came to live in Bowral with his family in 1911 and it is fitting that a museum of Australian cricket is established in his home town. Sir Donald's former home, which lies directly opposite the Oval, is owned by the Bradman Foundation. Under the supervision of Sir Donald, the cottage has been restored to its original form and retained as a historical site.

In October, 1989, the Bradman Pavilion was opened in the presence of Sir Donald and Lady Bradman. It has been the temporary home of the Museum collection. The Pavilion is open to the public daily and enjoys a visitation rate of more than 30,000 people each year. This figure is evidence of the public's respect for Sir Donald Bradman and the appreciation of cricket in our Australian lifestyle. When the second stage of the project is completed in 1995, the Pavilion will revert to a clubhouse.

The new Museum building will include exhibition galleries, theatrette, collection storage, library, museum shop and tea room. The permanent exhibitions will reflect the origins of cricket and the development of the game in Australia. Particular emphasis will be placed on Sir Donald Bradman and the outstanding period of cricket he represents. A series of temporary exhibitions will enable the Museum to remain in tune with current issues.

As well as operating the Museum, the Foundation conducts regular full-time live-in coaching clinics for children and sponsors the Bradman Scholarship scheme to Oxford and to an Australian university. These scholarships were launched by the former Prime Minister, the Hon R.J.L. Hawke AC, at the inaugural Spring Dinner in Sydney on October 13, 1989. The extensive upgrading of Bradman Oval to a first-class standard, and the formation of the Bradman Trust XI, has resulted in international, exhibition, local grade and village green cricket being played on the ground.

The subscription to the *"Friends of the Bradman Museum"* enables cricket enthusiasts to become more closely involved with the activities of the Museum by receiving a quarterly newsletter, *Boundary*, and invitations to all special events. Community involvement on Bradman Oval is evidenced by the Southern Highlands Arts Festival, Carols by Candlelight, the Southern Highlands Easter Cricket Festival and the construction of a new children's playground at Glebe Park.

The Foundation is a non profit public trust and all income generated is directed towards its objectives. Funding has come from private donation, corporate sponsorship, the Australian Federal Government and the New South Wales State Government. Sir Donald has given the project his full support and donated many objects from his personal possessions. At the Bradman Trust Spring Dinner in 1989, he said:

In my eyes the Bradman Trust has been created to honour and strengthen the game of cricket and that my name is merely the catalyst to give it birth and life. I cannot do other than give it my blessing and express my sincere thanks to all those people who are working so hard to make this dream become a reality and who have pledged themselves to make it a success.

The Trust's charter is to invoke the values and ideals that Sir Donald Bradman stood for. In doing so, it hopes to perpetuate the ideals not only of Sir Donald, but of the role of sporting excellence as a cultural force for all Australians.

*Richard Mulvaney,
Director, Bradman Museum,
July, 1994.*

England v Bradman XI, Bradman Oval, December, 1990.

The Bradman Pavilion northern view.

Sir Donald's former home, opposite Bradman Oval.

Part of the temporary display in the Bradman Pavilion.

Sir Donald Bradman AC. Artist: Bill Leak, 1989.

One of the most recent public photographs [above] of Sir Donald, taken at the official opening of the Bradman Stand at Adelaide Oval in 1990. This historic event not only further enshrined his name and greatness but was also fitting because his life, the oval, and South Australian cricket have been closely intertwined ever since Adelaide became his home in 1934.

Above: A match in progress at Adelaide Oval, one of the world's most beautiful cricket grounds.

Right: Inspecting one of his prize bats, on display at the State Library of South Australia in 1993.

Epilogue

INSPIRATION FOR A GROUNDSTAFF BOY

By Denis Compton

From *Compton On Cricketers Past and Present*, 1980.

Future generations may, I fear, become slightly sceptical about the legend and achievements of Donald George Bradman, and dismiss such scribblings as mine as exaggerated hero-worship, or a judgment warped and coloured by time. No single player, I can imagine it being said, could have been so impossibly gifted, or endowed with a temperament to match his extravagant ability. Or, it may be thought, the bowling of his age must have been ordinary - spanning twenty-one years? - and the field-placings naive.

The late Sir Pelham Warner was once asked by a group of players if W.G. Grace was as good as history made him out to be. His answer was: "Only those who played with and against him could have appreciated his true greatness and his impact on the game."

As with Grace, so with Bradman, who played havoc with all types of bowling, created records never likely to be surpassed, and fascinated all with the psychology of his make-up. He was unique, a batsman appearing not just once in a lifetime but once in the life of a game. His like will not be seen again, and I count it as my privilege that I was able to study his technique and methods from the closeness of slip and gully. I also came to know him as a man and in my experience The Don was far from "a solitary man with a solitary aim", as an eminent critic claimed.

If any should doubt the crushing power of his strokes please, I beg you, take the word of one who fielded on the boundary to him and watched a round red bullet repeatedly pass at unstoppable speed, and placed with such precision that I had no earthly chance of getting within reach.

When I first played against The Don I was a precocious twenty-year-old. My mind was flooded with mixed sensations of awe, respect and plain curiosity - one could imagine a recruit to Winston Churchill's war-time Cabinet undergoing the same emotions. The mere presence of the greatest cricketer the world had known on the same field as myself was unnerving, and after encountering Bradman in two home series and one in Australia, I never lost the sense of being in contact with history.

Far from breeding contempt, familiarity nourished my wonder at everything Bradman did. He was a living miracle, defying comparison with any other player before, during or since his time, and an early description of him stood the test of time. Jack Ryder, a former captain of Australia, was asked how Bradman played. He replied, "He just belts the hell out of anything within reach." He did just that, and unlike Jack Hobbs and Victor Trumper, never threw his wicket away when he thought he had had enough.

I suppose my attitude to Bradman had its roots in my sporting background and my immersion in the game. My father and I once took a No 13 bus from our home at Hendon to Lord's in 1930 to watch the phenomenon everyone talked about, but I am ashamed to admit that my memory of the occasion is blurred and I remember nothing of The Don. At least I didn't suffer the disappointment I had on a Bank Holiday at The Oval when Hobbs, my idol, was bowled for a modest 22, though there was a wondrous exhibition of cutting from his partner, Andy Sandham, the memory of which excites me to this day.

In 1934 Bradman was back in England, and I had been a groundstaff boy at Lord's for two years. Sometimes the leading players of Middlesex might stroll to the Nursery to cast critical eyes on young hopefuls like me, and the conversation inevitably turned to Bradman, who seemed to score at will and at a fantastic pace. Bradman was the constant subject. His very name was magic, and the inimitable "Patsy" Hendren, who had played in The Don's first Test at Brisbane in 1928, fed me with every scrap of detail. "Patsy" scored 169, England won by 675 runs, and the way Australia were ground in the dust was said to sour and fashion Bradman's attitude to the way a Test had to be played.

Unfortunately contact with the foremost players was seldom possible for groundstaff boys - the lowest form of cricketing life! - and I was able to see Bradman in action only briefly as I sold scorecards during the famous Second Test, when the late Hedley Verity took 14 wickets in a day and 15 all told. Frank Chester, the umpire, told me an overnight storm left a patch at one end no bigger than the circumference of a frying-pan. It was enough for Verity.

Bradman had been out when the game was resumed for a small but brilliant 36, but, oddly, he served as an inspiration to me even in failure. Australia followed on, and I was at once fascinated and impressed at the way Bradman met aggressive bowling with a counter-attack. Though he gave a skied catch to Les Ames at the wicket I could not forget his positive approach in what was really a hopeless situation, and there can be no doubt that a firm Compton philosophy which was to serve me well throughout my career was conceived on that occasion. He made me realise that in the final analysis attack is the best form of defence, and it is better to take the fight to the enemy than be dominated by him. I have never changed my opinion that the successes gained by intelligent assault far outnumber the failures.

It was invariably held against Bradman that, in contrast to Hobbs, he was not a master in all conditions and was vulnerable to the turning ball, particularly with his unconventional grip, if it was leaving the bat. Aren't we all? Verity did not share the conventional view, and I am inclined to agree with his opinion that

The Don's attitude on sticky pitches was a form of protest.

He was never one to hold a weak belief on any subject, and he was very much against uncovered pitches. The argument was that Lindrum and Davis would never be expected to perform on a lumpy billiards table, and it was wrong to play cricket on a pitch open to the vagaries of the weather, besides being grossly unfair to one side. As a batsman I agreed, and for my part I find it inconceivable that The Don, who batted with ultimate perfection and saw the ball on the bat as late as it was possible, could not have devised a technique for wet conditions if he had put his mind to the problem.

It seemed a matter of principle to him not to overcome a bad wicket, and he shrugged his shoulders like a renowned actor enduring bad acoustics at a one-night stand. Nor did I pay much attention to the criticism that he would hold himself back and expose his less fortunate and less talented team-mates to the torments of a drying surface. To me that would be simple logic, and totally in the interest of his side.

To The Don there was no mountain high enough. His cricket was planned to the last detail, and I confess that on the occasions I bowled to him I was in near-despair. Every basic requirement of batting was there in abundance - the lightning reflexes of brain and eye, footwork which would not have come amiss in the Bolshoi ballet, a delicate balance and the self-confidence springing from a belief in his own dazzling ability.

He had a marvellous gift of getting into position quicker than any batsman I have ever seen, played the ball very late, and was never off balance, or stretching out of control. With his judgment of length he would make his quick decision and play either back or forward without hesitation. Brain and body were in perfect harmony. I could understand the temptation to regard him as simply a run-machine with such built-in powers of concentration and personal drive as to be incapable of human error. Certainly he lacked the charm at the crease of an Alan Kippax or a Tom Graveney. He was not in that sense a stylist. But he was fallible to the occasional error for the simple reason that he made his runs at a fantastic rate and never refused a challenge. Often I would look at the scoreboard and be surprised to find he had twice as many runs as I figured he had scored. He was forever finding the gaps and taking the singles and the twos.

Modern bowling and field placings might have cramped and confined him to a degree, but would not have finally defeated him. It might have taken him longer to make his scores, but he would not have been utterly shackled or have allowed the bowlers to dictate their terms. Instead of being 300 at the end of that remarkable day at Headingley he would possibly have been 220 or 240 not out. In any case with the slow over rates he would not have received anything like the number of deliveries.

With his uncanny ball sense Bradman could master any ball game. He flirted with lawn tennis for a time and doubtless would have become a champion. Within weeks of starting billiards he made century breaks, and he had the same success with golf and squash.

His cricket was uniquely Bradman. No coaching manual was intended for him, and despite what is said to the contrary I am sure that had he been born English no coach would have dared to interfere with him. His grip would have doubtless caused some consternation. Both hands were turned over the handle with the fingers of the left hidden from the bowler. The swift answer to those who said it was wrong was in his murderous hooking and cutting. The only doubt raised by his unorthodox grip was his cover drive and his defence against the ball leaving the bat.

But I cannot honestly recall him as an ineffective cover driver, and his record scarcely suggests that he was ever technically handicapped! If he once reached 30 or so the fielding side were thankful if he was satisfied with a single century.

He gathered runs at such a speed that it was impossible to set a field for him, and it occurred to me at times that he had a private game with a slow-moving fielder or with the opposing captain. His placements were so exact that he could have a fielder moving backwards and forwards from one position to another. There was, in fact, no precise field setting for The Don because he was able to improvise brilliantly, as I found to my cost at Sydney in the 1946-7 series.

Bradman's hook was pure magic. There has not been a batsman I have seen able to match his special skill with a shot that gets so many able batsmen in difficulties. Today's batsmen, plagued with the obsessive use of the bumper and the short-pitched delivery, ought to study every action picture and film they can get of Bradman playing the hook. Never once did I see him hook in the air, and, unlike even the best who aim for deep square or fine of square, Bradman whacked the ball in the direction of mid-on. Bradman was different because he was fractionally quicker in picking up the ball, and was in position faster. His secret was to pick up the flight path and pitch of the ball so soon that he actually seemed to be in position and waiting for it from the moment it left the bowler's hand. He was unsurpassed in his timing and execution, and I am certain bowlers would have been disinclined to use the bouncer too often against him.

Bradman was the unwitting cause of the so-called bodyline form of attack. If ever there was a back-handed compliment to genius it was the invention and employment of bodyline. Douglas Jardine and his ally Harold Larwood roughly halved Bradman's output and average to 396 runs at an average of 56.57. By Bradman's standards a failure, but even with seven fielders on the leg side and the ball screaming at his head at a speed of ninety miles an hour or so Bradman improvised with shots placed on the off side. He also had a tennis-style smash back over the bowler's head.

The cut was one of The Don's favourite shots. As with his hook, the ball was kept on the ground. Anything fractionally short of a length or over-pitched was murderously assaulted, and his moral ascendancy over the bowlers was enough to give him an advantage before a ball was bowled. Understandably, Bradman's reputation was enough to send a chill down the spine, and bowlers knew they had to pitch an immaculate line and length or they were set for merciless punishment. I suffered a definite sense of inferiority on the occasions I bowled to him. I admit I was an unpredictable slow left-arm spinner with an inclination to experiment. But precisely because I felt I must not bowl a bad ball to Bradman, I invariable ended up doing so. And he never failed to hit a bad ball.

Memories of Bradman

BILL BROWN
Australian Test batsman

I often recall one particular match involving Don. It was for NSW against Victoria at the Sydney Cricket Ground in 1934. Jack Fingleton and I had opened the innings. In those days the new ball came in at 200 irrespective of the number of overs. Don came in when I needed about 30 to get my hundred. He said: "Bill, we want to get you your 100 before the new ball comes on." So he proceeded to quietly pick up singles here and there while I went on and managed to get my hundred. I was then 103, he was about 15 or 16. When I was 128 he was 129. It was a very good Victorian attack. Ebeling was the Captain and the side included good bowlers like McCormick and Fleetwood-Smith but he hit them all over the place. Another time we were batting together in Brisbane; it was only my first or second time there. I was having trouble with Ron Oxenham, who was quite a good Queensland bowler. Don came up and said he would take the bowling for a while to give me a spell, which he did. After a few overs I was able to settle down a bit and get some runs. It showed he wasn't a selfish player immersed in his own activities.

He was a splendid runner between the wickets, very fast. The first time I ever played with him was in what was called a Super Grade match in Sydney where they picked teams from the north, south, east and west. It was 1931 and Don had just arrived back from England and, of course, was the hero of Australia. We were batting together and having a pretty good old time, hitting the ball and running, when at the end of one over he came down the wicket and called me up. I wondered what he was going to say. I thought he might say: "Bill, you're going pretty well, keep it up and you'll go places." Instead of that he said: "Bill, I've never had the pleasure of playing with you before. Do you think you could call when you're going to run?" The next time I called for a single I think you could have heard me up on the Blue Mountains.

There was a story around he couldn't bat on wet wickets. I batted with him twice on wet wickets. One was in 1932-1933 against Jardine's team at the Sydney Cricket Ground. Batting against Larwood and Verity he got 70 odd runs and batted beautifully. Everyone else got out. The second time was in the Lord's Test of 1938 when he scored a century on a wicket that wasn't too good at all. The ball was jumping all over the place, especially from Ken Farnes. I stayed with him for a while but it was too much for me. I was full of admiration for his innings. To see the way he handled the conditions was a real eye-opener. Those two innings proved to me he could get runs on wet as well as dry wickets.

One thing about his batting that always impressed me was that he would stand almost perfectly still while the bowler was approaching the wicket. He didn't shuffle around the crease. Once the ball was bowled he sized it up in a flash and would explode into action. There is no question he brought wonderful physical ability to play the game but he also brought this tremendous mental application and concentration. He could analyse the game much more deeply and quickly than the average player. He controlled the game so much when he was at the wicket.

He was so popular in his day you would get say a few thousand before lunch, but if he was going to bat after lunch you would get another 15 or 20 thousand people, even more, along not so much to watch the cricket but to watch Bradman bat. He was the best value for money in sporting entertainment that there was to be had. And he very seldom disappointed people. People who didn't normally go to the cricket went to watch Bradman bat. Jack Fingleton and I would open the innings and, with a bit of luck, we'd bat to lunchtime. But if you stayed in too much longer after lunch the crowd got restless because you were batting in Bradman's time. If you got hit on the pads, not only would the bowler and the fielders appeal but also the whole crowd would appeal in the hope you'd be out. If you were given out, you'd get the most tremendous applause as you walked off, not because you'd batted well, but that you were out of the road so Bradman could come in. It only happened with Bradman. He transformed the game into something entirely different.

When he first came in he would get a run off the first ball if he possibly could, and 99 times out of a hundred he did. Everyone knew he would go for the single, his batting partner, bowlers, fielders and the crowd. He would look around and tap the ball just wide of the fieldsman and run. The crowd would let out a roar when he did this and from then on he'd be the whole focus of attention. His first 50 would usually be scored in 60 or 70 minutes, the next one would come down to about 50 minutes and the next one would be down further still and so on. He scored so very quickly all the time without hitting the ball into the air.

The same skills and principles applied to batting then as they do now and he had those skills in excelsis. I see no reason why he wouldn't control the game now as he did then. You can only do certain things with a cricket ball. Don was able to handle everything the bowlers tried with consummate ease back in those days and I really can't see any reason why he wouldn't do the same now. Playing with him was a great privilege. There was an aura about him that is difficult to describe. You could feel that once he came out to the wicket the game changed. It became more than just a game of cricket. I suppose it would be like walking onto the stage with Sir Laurence Olivier. You were part of something that was happening far beyond the ordinary.

ARTHUR MORRIS
Australian Test batsman.

If you didn't see Bradman bat you didn't realise how good he was. I always quote Stan McCabe who was one the greatest players I ever saw. Talking about Bradman he once pointed up to the ceiling and said: "He's up there and the rest of us are down here." I don't live in the past, I can assure you, but when I hear people comparing him with players of later years I realise they didn't see Bradman so they didn't know how good he was.

One of the many amazing things about Bradman was his memory. He remembered everything. In the Fifth Test against England at The Oval in 1948 I was fielding just near the umpire when Denis Compton came out to bat and Bradman shifted me about five yards finer. Lindwall bowled a bouncer and Compton hit the ball straight to me and I caught it. I went up to Bradman and said: "Why did you move me?" He replied: "Denis played the same shot down in that direction off Ernie McCormick in 1938."

SAM LOXTON
Australian Test player

The greatest compliment I believe that has ever been paid to a cricketer will be found in a couple of lines of small type in the 1939 edition of *The Wisden Cricketers' Almanack*, buried in the midst of the story about the Fifth Test at The Oval in 1938, which was scheduled as a timeless Test. These lines said : "Indeed, Hammond probably would not have closed the innings during the tea interval on the third day but for the mishap to the opposing captain." England were 7 for 903 and Bradman had fractured a bone in his ankle while bowling and took no further part in the match. Just imagine it, here we have a captain who isn't going to declare until someone breaks a bone in his ankle, and the score is 903. It goes to show the awe in which Bradman was held.

Cricket followers of today have no conception of just how good Bradman was. When people try to compare him with the modern players they tend to overlook some very important aspects of his career, for example, they forget that in his 52 Test matches over 22 years he never once batted on a covered wicket. After the start of play in those 52 Tests the pitches were subject to the elements. People who never saw him play don't realise the tremendous power, timing and precision he displayed in playing his shots.

The most memorable and the most incredible shot I ever saw Bradman play was after the Tea adjournment on Saturday, February the 25th, 1949, during the Kippax-Oldfield Testimonial at the Sydney Cricket Ground, his last at the SCG. He was in his 41st year and had not played since his Testimonial in Melbourne at the beginning of December. Only two players knew what was about to happen. Don was batting at the Randwick end. Keith Miller commenced an over from the Noble stand end. As I handed him the ball, relayed to me at mid off, he said: "Sammy, the little feller doesn't like 'em short . I'm going to give him one." He did. It pitched off stump, took off and Gil Langley took it over his head. It went past The Don's nose by six inches. I can see him now. He looked up the pitch and smiled. As I gave Keith the ball again he said: "Told ya. Let's see how he handles this one." Believe me "this one" was equally vicious. It pitched middle and leg. Don got inside the line and hit that hook shot. He rolled his wrists and from nose to ground the ball travelled less than 10 feet. It hit the fence in the gap between the Members' Stand and the Ladies' pavilion, heading for the turnstiles and Anzac Parade. I want to tell you that had the fence not been there, the ball probably would have finished up in Taylors Square. Keith's comment: "I take it back." The look on his face was unbelievable. When people ask me how Bradman would have fared against modern bowlers I tell them that story. He would have slaughtered them the same as he did bowlers during his playing days. He was a genius.

Take his innings when he made his Test record 334 in 1930. He goes in during the first over of the day when Jackson is out. By lunch he's 100, by tea he's 200 and by the end of the day he's 309 not out. What else can you say about a man like that? The greatest privilege of my sporting career has been to be associated with Bradman who was not only a genius on the cricket field but a great bloke, and a man of enormous integrity.

JACK FINGLETON
Australian Test player and author

The world has not seen his equal, nor anybody approaching his equal, in the consistency and degree of his big scores. I particularly stress the word consistency. Some of aesthetic taste might have preferred the cultured charm of a Kippax or a Jackson to Bradman's flaying piece; I saw Macartney and knew his genius to be of a different mould to that of Bradman. Repute also had Trumper to be of a different mould; but, in the sheer consistency and robust profligacy of their respective arts, Bradman far outshone all others, the English eras of Grace, Maclaren, Hayward and Hobbs not excluded.

Other individuals might have been noted for fast footwork, unerring judgment or brilliant eyesight, Bradman possessed all of these; but, if there was one faculty which made him superior to others, it was in being able to judge, almost as soon as the ball left the bowler's hand, the length, spin and merit of that particular delivery. Therein lay much of his greatness - a quicker brain, a quicker judgment than any other batsman I have seen. But a batsman does not place himself on a pinnacle such as Bradman occupied by virtue of any one, two or three outstanding gifts. Bradman was richly endowed in all that went towards making him the champion and none more so than his twinkling, magical feet.

Bradman at the wicket was completely at ease and at rest until the ball began its apologetic advance towards him. His lithe, compact body was a power-house of latent electricity until the switch of the ball released was turned, and then his brightness flashed in all directions. His feet took him into immediate position to offset swerve, swing or break bowling; his running feet took him three and even four yards up the pitch to slow bowling to kill the break and take advantage of the gap in the field which his eye had detected. He was at his best in making the placement of a field look foolish.

He was the genius absolute. To bat with him was an education and a revelation, not given by any other batsman of the period. Great artists like Trumper and Macartney varied the direction of the shot for sheer artistic satisfaction, but Bradman was implacable. He was more interested in runs than art.

Excerpt from *Cricket Crisis*, 1946.

BERT OLDFIELD
Australian Test wicket keeper

Granted he has a quick eye, fleetness of foot, uncanny anticipation and unlimited patience, but behind these obvious qualities lie a will and mind that govern all his movements. His development of stroke play and self-control as he progressed in the game was to me amazing. I have seen him, when dismissed for small scores, quietly sitting in the dressing room, like a student pondering the cause of his mistake, and thinking out effective methods of overcoming the error. He has always been a keen critic of his own defects and this, no doubt, is the secret behind all his greatness and success.

- Bert Oldfield, 1938.

C.B. FRY
England Test cricketer
Writing about his first sighting of Bradman in 1934:

Until yesterday I'd never seen Bradman play. Of course, I was immensely interested in him, and asked the experts to explain him to me. I got nothing but the usual adjectives, and these cloud any subject. My madame told me: "He's a little man with fairy feet, who watches the ball." That did convey something. This Don Bradman, we all know, is a marvel. Merely on figures. But the interesting point is why and how. I will tell you. He's beautifully built for physical fine art: by conformation an athlete of the lightweight type. Many great batsmen have not been athletic.

Bradman has a gem of a body for batsmanship, conformation perfect: hence perfect poise. A bundle, beautifully shaped, of what the Greeks called harmony. He is light armed, free and ever so quick with his bat. He need not begin his stroke till the last fraction of a second. Hence, he is never compromised before he sees, actually sees, the ball right up to its full development. It is a simple point: moderate giants play at the ball as they figure it will come. This little master plays at the ball as it is. The difference between mastery and mediocrity - with a bat.

He has lovely wrists - that grace in batting. He moves on his feet ever so neatly and ever so easily in good time. He is poised on the ball of the feet, not the flat. Like a good dancer. More, he does trust his eye utterly. Not afraid really to wait and see. Remains, the psychic side. And this is a big plus for your Don.

This young man owes half his perfection to an outright power of concentration. Native or acquired, it's the sine qua non of mastery. You can see it in his face. Firm little mouth, winner's chin. He has the quality as a settled habit and no doubt subconscious. His sheet anchor. He has a humour too. A great asset. If only the Australian Board of Control would let him, he'd amuse us with words as well as shock us with runs. I like the little demon.

ALEC BEDSER
England Test bowler

Bradman was technically perfect in defence. Also, he had amazingly quick footwork and eye and masterful back play. Bowlers were left with no possible margin for error, for anything short was murderously cut or pulled. Given the chance he would readily use that lethal pull the first ball he received, as Surrey discovered at The Oval in 1948. Stuart Surridge, Surrey's enthusiastic skipper, was the bowler and that admirable all-rounder, Jack Parker, was at short leg. Surridge pitched short and before Jack had time to move the ball had hit the fence. Bradman mostly struck his pull square of the wicket, the power was incredible and the ball hardly ever left the turf.

One sign of his control was the absence of uppish shots and one of his dictums was: "If you hit the ball on the ground there's less chance of getting out." How disarmingly simple this sounds. If genius is the art of doing the simple things properly, Bradman was a classic example. While lesser players tend to create complications and mental exhaustion, Bradman knew precisely what he intended to do, and went his way with a minimum of fuss. He always kept the score moving. I would glance at the scoreboard thinking he had been tolerably contained, and be surprised to see how quickly he had progressed. He always ran the first run as fast as he could, and expected to get two to third man. While the average batsman would look for no more than a single The Don aimed to get two. Pressure was at once put on the fielder, and looking up he might fumble or throw wildly and end by conceding an extra run. The Don's placing was superb and produced a non-stop flow of singles and twos.

When I first played against him I was taken aback by his speed between the wickets, even at the end of a long and arduous innings. No matter where the field was set Bradman refused to be tied down, and he still found gaps with consummate ease. His placements were an exact science and were a constant source of concern to me, particularly before I learned where to set my field. A bowler can be annoyed by the steady seepage of singles, and I think Bradman enjoyed this battle of wits with the field.

Once The Don was set he manipulated the field like a master puppeteer. He was so quickly into position with those tiny feet [at least by my standard] of his that he could change his stroke with impunity. I commend every batsman, young or old, to study old films of Bradman in action. They would marvel at his use of the crease, the speed and certainty of his footwork, and perhaps absorb the truth that intelligent attack is the best form of defence.

Before I went to Australia I heard many contradictory stories about him. I was determined to take him as I found him. I can truthfully say I have never found him anything but a thoughtful, kind and considerate friend and a hard, but fair opponent.
- An excerpt from *Cricket Choice*, by Alec Bedser, 1981.

WALTER HAMMOND
England Test Captain

He had a capacity I have never seen equalled in any other cricketer of docketing his cricket in one part of the mind and never letting any other thought even intrude there. That is a quality of concentration on the game that everyone must develop, who is to be successful, but not many of us, I think, have the ruthless capacity of a Bradman to perfect such a power as he did.

I was forced to admire the cool way Don batted. On one or two occasions, when he was well set, and when he saw me move a fieldsman, he would raise his gloved hand to me in mock salute, and then hit the next ball exactly over the place from which the man had just been moved. Reluctantly I had to admit once more that he was out of the ordinary run of batsmen - a genius!
- *Walter Hammond, 1952.*

SID BARNES
Australian Test player
Writing after his world record breaking partnership
with Bradman against England at the SCG in 1946:

Bradman is most encouraging when you bat with him. He keeps up a running commentary in between overs and is full of information about what the other captain and his bowlers are thinking and trying to do. He never misses a beat. He too, is a diplomat. He kept telling me during that partnership how the whole Test rested upon me.

I began to feel, after a while, that I was carrying the House of Bradman as well as Australia's cricketing fortunes on my shoulders. I am unlike Bradman in one respect. A century always satisfied me, no matter what type of match it was. I was out soon after for the same tally as Bradman - 234. I had better clear that up. Lots of people have asked me whether I deliberately threw my wicket away at 234. The answer is yes. We had set a new world-record for the fifth-wicket of 405. R.E. Foster had the record Test score on the Sydney ground of 287 but the previous best by an Australian was Sydney Gregory's 201. I passed that first, then Bradman, and when I got to 234 I knew another single would give me the record on my own. But I preferred to have my name associated with Don's in holding the joint record. I worshipped him. He could do nothing wrong as far as I was concerned.

We both had a lot in common. He had also given me much advice. And so, with all this at the back of my mind, I hit one high above my head and walked out. In cricket's language I tossed my innings away. Bradman was roaring when I got into the dressing room, but only with the pain of having adhesive tape ripped off thigh muscles. He grinned at me. "Well done, Bagga", he said, "you have done a great job for Australia". "You didn't do so bad yourself," I grinned back at him.

It Isn't Cricket, by Sid Barnes, 1963.

BILL O'REILLY
Australian Test bowler
Writing about their first clash in first-class cricket.

All those who never had the animated experience of bowling at him have, so it seems, been most impressed with his speed and cleverness in leaving the crease and moving well down pitch in search of his prey. To those people I hasten to give the assurance that the forward move was not the secret of this maestro's success.

Hidden securely in his mental clockwork was an extraordinary facility for summing up the length and speed of a delivery simultaneously, so it seemed, with the ball's release from the bowler's hand. This gave him the immeasurable advantage of deciding immediately whether to move onto the front or the back foot. You can take it from me, who bowled at every single batsman on the international first-class scene between 1931 and 1938, that the toughest batting proposition facing any bowler is the discerning batsman who knows just when to use back-foot play.

One of my first jobs in facing up to an unknown batsman was to find out without delay how secure he was when forced onto the back foot in defending his wicket. If he showed me the slightest sign that his technique in that regard was faulty I couldn't get the ball back again quickly enough to concentrate on the dissection of the case. Give me a batsman, I used to think, who could not defend stoutly on the back foot, and I would have been prepared to give a written guarantee that I would get him out at last once every over I bowled at him.

You can therefore imagine my surprise and unbounded admiration for the young Bradman when I observed him going onto his back foot so confidently, not only to defend, but also to take many runs on the leg side with a new leg glance and a powerful hook fine of square leg.

As a batsman, he was an undoubted genius. Bowling at him was a grand experience for a thoughtful bowler. He seemed to have a ready and highly reliable answer for everything a bowler tried. He had an insatiable appetite for runs. It seemed that run-getting was his ingrained method of self-expression and not lacking any of the innate tendency of self-assertiveness, he expressed himself long and loud. There was no escaping the Bradman bat when it was charged with the responsibility of smashing down all opposition.

- *Tiger,* by Bill O'Reilly, 1985.

RAY LINDWALL
Australian Test fast bowler

Before I even set eyes on him I was a Bradman fan, and, after watching him play for my local St. George club, I became a still more fervent admirer. Since then I have played with Don many times. In too many instances boyhood idols have feet of clay, but nothing in the passing years has caused me to lose any of my youthful admiration for Australia's only cricketing Knight.

During a reign as cricket's king which lasted nearly 20 years Bradman was the bulwark of every Australian side. His deeds and consistency were nothing short of amazing, but of equal value was the feeling of supreme confidence his presence gave to the rest of the eleven. Even in moments of crisis the atmosphere in the Australian dressing room was always that "everything is bound to work out right, The Don is playing".

I am only one of the men who regretted his departure from the cricket scene. From my earliest days as a devoted Bradman fan on the St George ground he had remained a hero to me, but from the first time I met him as a cricketer he had treated me exactly as an equal. I never heard him say a word of criticism about anyone else in the game, player or official, and I never heard him complain about an umpire's decision.

Even when the majority of those watching thought the umpire had made a mistake, Bradman would return to the dressing room, sit down quietly to unbuckle his pads and go for his bath without a suggestion of dissatisfaction or disagreement with the ruling.

- *Flying Stumps,* by Ray Lindwall, 1954.

SIR ROBERT MENZIES
Australian Prime Minister

I write as a looker-on; as a lover of the game and its history and its beauty and unforgettable pictures which it etches upon the visual memory. For twenty years I have been Don Bradman's beneficiary, for he is the greatest batsman, the most devastating stroke-maker, and the shrewdest and most concentrated tactician I ever hope to see. He is, of course, not without his critics; he has succeeded too gigantically to escape them. He has had faults, no doubt, but they are merely the defects inherent in those positive qualities which have given him his pre-eminence. In him we have witnessed the supreme cricketing combination; the quick eye ["sees the ball three yards sooner than any of the rest of us," Bill Ponsford once said to me], the instantaneous muscular response, the incisive and flashing intelligence. For mark you, Don Bradman is a man of uncommon intelligence from whatever angle you consider him. He believes in the virtue of concentrating all your mind upon the job in hand. He therefore plays to win.

Once or twice I have thought that this ruthless quality might have been tempered with a little mercy; but reflection has almost always brought me back to the recognition that intense concentration IS a cardinal virtue, so rare that for its sake even much might be forgiven. As a pavilion lover of the greatest of all games, I have balanced up the Bradman Account and hereby acknowledge that so long as my memory lasts I shall owe him that which I can never repay.

R.C. ROBERTSON-GLASGOW
English County cricketer and noted cricket writer.

Don Bradman will bat no more against England, and two contrary feelings dispute within us: relief, that our bowlers will no longer be oppressed by this phenomenon; regret, that a miracle has been removed from among us. So must ancient Italy have felt when she heard of the death of Hannibal.

Bradman was a business-cricketer. About his batting there was no style for style's sake. If there was to be any charm, that was for the spectator to find or miss. It was not Bradman's concern. His aim was the making of runs, and he made them in staggering and ceaseless profusion. He seemed to have eliminated error, to have perfected the mechanism of the stroke. He was, as near as man batting may be, the flawless engine. Man, by his nature, cannot bear perfection in his fellow. The very fact that something is being done which had been believed to be impossible goads and irritates. It is but a short step from annoyance to envy, and Bradman has never been free of envy's attack.

So, when, first in 1930, he reeled off the centuries, single, double and treble, there were not wanting those who compared him unfavourably with other great ones - Trumper, Ranjitsinhji, Hobbs, Macartney. And Bradman's answer was more runs. Others, perhaps, could have made them, but they didn't.

No one before had ever been quite so fit, quite so ruthless. It was a coolly considered policy. Cricket was not to be his hobby, his off-hours delight. It was to be his life and his living. He did not

mean to be just one of the stars, but the sun itself. Never was such an ambition achieved and sustained. Never was the limelight so unwaveringly on one man in one game. To set a standard was unique. To keep it was a miracle.

Bradman's place as a batsman is among the few who have been blessed with genius. He was the most wonderful run-scorer the game has yet known, and no batsman in our own time has so highly excited expectation and so rarely disappointed it.

- Wisden Cricketers' Almanack, on Bradman's retirement in 1949.

Don Bradman has as many angles as a polygon; and, like that monster of geometry Don was born to perplex students; and bowlers. Don and Jack Hobbs overlapped, just. I had the luck to play against both a time or two and to watch both more than a time or two. On "bad" pitches - sticky, dusty, broken, call them as you please - I'd put Jack ahead of all contemporaries. But on "good" pitches - that is to bowlers 22 yards of dumb hell - Don was the non pareil. I'd rather have watched Wally Hammond twenty years back, off-driving, and I'd rather have seen Stan McCabe to the real fast stuff.

But you go round the great ones and you come back to Don and his figures. You can't answer them. They don't speak. They exist; and will exist; a monument more enduring than bronze. When I first saw Bradman, in England, he was an exquisitely heartless murderer of bowlers. He sliced them, into very small pieces. He danced on them neatly and conclusively. There'll never be another innings like his 334 against England at Leeds in 1930, never.

- The London Observer, 1948.

HAROLD LARWOOD
English Test bowler, 1928 to 1933

There seemed to be no answer to Bradman's batting in 1930. He did all the things you didn't want him to. You could bowl on the off trying to get him to lift one or give a catch behind and he'd pull you hard to the leg fence. He had the quickest eye of any batsman I ever met. There seemed only one way to get him out - tire him out. But he never seemed to tire. His stamina and concentration were extraordinary.

Don was cruel the way he flogged you. He seemed to have a computer-type approach, never giving anything away and always able to go his own inexorable way. He jumped down the pitch to the bowler when he felt like it which was most of the time.

Nobody watching the majority of the "pat ball" batsmen of today can have any idea what Don was like. Good length stuff went to the boundary like a bullet. He used all the shots in the book, and a few that weren't. He used to lean back and cut you or move into position for a leg shot even before the ball was delivered.

He was the most challenging batsman I ever bowled to. I have no hesitation in saying Bradman is the greatest batsman in my lifetime, I doubt if there will ever be another like him.

- Excerpt from The Larwood Story
by Harold Larwood with Kevin Perkins.

ALAN McGILVRAY
NSW Sheffield Shield player and ABC radio commentator

There was a calculating ruthlessness to Bradman's batting. He would rarely talk to anybody on the field. He always seemed to be in total communion with himself, his concentration maintained at levels which allowed no intrusion whatever from those around him. He knew the value of his own ability. He knew bowlers would devise all manner of schemes and plans to try to dismiss him. The very stature his extraordinary skill gave him demanded he concentrate that much harder than anybody else. He communicated by means of his bat. If he received a particularly good ball, he would acknowledge by defending, without a word. If a ball deserved to be hit, he would whip it away, again without a word. He was like a machine. But he was an aggressive machine. He had a high regard for the entertainment value of cricket. He saw no percentage in grinding out an innings.

Bradman had almost perfect co-ordination of eye, brain, and body that set him apart. He had powerful, sinewy legs and forearms, and small feet - he took only size five in footwear - that allowed him to shuffle into position with lightning speed. His reflexes were sharp and true, his eyesight piercing. But above all he had a mind which was quicker than any other I have known to size up where a ball would pitch, its speed, its movement and its worth.

In terms of sheer power Bradman was never in the mould of men like Walter Hammond, Garfield Sobers or Graeme Pollock. But he valued control above power. His placement was uncanny, his range of shots unmatched. He minimised mistakes and timed his shots immaculately. When he unwound into a pull shot or leaned back to cut, he hit with great flourish. In essence, he simply did everything right.

His record as a cricketer and his standing as a sportsman of a rare kind have proved impervious to anything that would seek to undermine them. If anything time has enhanced his greatness. Considering the unarguable weight of figures that stand behind him, and the results his batting achieved, it is extraordinary to look back on Bradman's career and count the critics who continually looked for flaws. Either he didn't hold the bat right, or he hit across the line too much or he was not so good on bad wickets. There were those who claimed he was not a team man; that he distanced himself from his contemporaries. There always seemed to be somebody having a go at him about something.

The great England opener Herbert Sutcliffe, for instance, once qualified Bradman's greatness by saying he was the best batsman he had seen "on good wickets". And so many of Bradman's critics felt compelled to say things like "he was not as good as Victor Trumper on wet wickets". If that is so, Trumper must have been absolutely magnificent. Others would bring up Archie Jackson, who came into the Test side about the same time as Bradman and hit 164 on debut, and claim that, had he lived, he would have been a better player. How they could possibly know that escapes me. But throughout his career, Bradman had to suffer those who would seek to minimise his greatness. It has always been a queer trait in the Australian character

that we feel compelled to claw at the state of those who excel. To cut down the tall poppies, as it were. So many, so often, were only too ready to carp at Don Bradman for inconsequentials as diverse as the clothes he wore or the way he spoke. The constancy of such irritating criticism took its toll.

He tended to build a wall around himself. He developed an aloofness and distance in his bearing that made him hard to know. There were other factors responsible for this intensely private side to his nature. Bradman was never a great mixer in accepted cricketing terms. You would rarely find him at the bar, drinking with the boys. He kept to himself as a basic requirement of captaincy as he saw it. Before the war, when he captained essentially the men he grew up with, that distance counted against him. They saw it as loftiness, a setting apart that many resented. I suspect through those times, however, Bradman's success as a batsman, as much as his manner, encouraged the disdain of some of his contemporaries. Throughout his cricketing life he was the subject of much envy. Making it worse was a certain untouchable quality Bradman had about him. No matter how much people attacked him, he rarely reacted. Critics found him as difficult to ruffle as bowlers.

Just a couple of years ago, Sir Donald Bradman did me the honour of asking me to launch his biography, *Bradman*. I was very touched by the invitation. I said at the book launching Bradman was a legend. There seems always to be a certain mystery surrounding men whose stature is such that they stand above their environment. Bradman has always had that mystery. Sometimes it has been misunderstood. But his record as a cricketer and his standing as a sportsman of a rare kind have proved impervious to anything that would seek to undermine them.

If anything, time has enhanced his greatness. Bradman's contribution to cricket over that twenty-year period is inestimable. As a batsman he had no peer. As a captain he achieved exactly what he set out to achieve. And he did it his way. Don Bradman was very much the master of his own destiny.

-Excerpts from *The Game Is Not the Same*,
by Alan McGilvray with Norm Tasker.

LORD TENNYSON
England Test cricketer
Writing after Bradman's 304 in the 1934 Test at Lord's.

You may search the records of international cricket as you will, and you will not find a greater feat than he performed at Lord's. His effort may not be valued by his colossal score; it was the iron discipline of the man, the sacrifice of his real self for his country, his unsuspected patience, the scorn with which he answered his critics, that was the wonder, the delight, the masterfulness of his innings; his defiance, his magnetism - that was the mightiness of his conquest.

There have been occasions when sticklers for what we are pleased to call style have professed to see flaws in his batsmanship. I make bold to say that Bradman has all the strokes, and then some. He is competent to play any game - the game that, in its dash and gusto, is typically Bradmanesque, or one that tells of the complete scholar. And in whatever guise he compels admiration. He is no run-getting machine: Bradman is a genius.

Scoreboard

STATISTICAL RECORD OF SIR DONALD BRADMAN'S CAREER

ALL MATCHES

	Innings	Not Out	Runs	Aggregate	Average	Centuries
All matches	669	107	452*	50,751	90.27	211
First-class	338	43	452*	28,067	95.1	117
Second-class	331	64	320*	22,664	84.8	94
Test cricket	80	10	334	6,996	99.94	29
Tests v England	63	7	334	5,028	89.78	19
Sheffield Shield	96	15	452*	8,926	110.19	36
Grade cricket	93	17	503	6,598	86.8	28

SCORES IN FIRST-CLASS CRICKET IN AUSTRALIA

Season	Innings	Not Out	Highest Score	Runs	Average	Centuries
1927-28	10	1	154	416	46.22	2
1928-29	24	6	340*	1,690	93.88	7
1929-30	16	2	452*	1,586	113.28	5
1930-31	18	-	258	1,422	79.00	5
1931-32	13	1	299*	1,403	116.91	7
1932-33	21	2	238	1,171	61.63	3
1933-34	11	2	253	1,192	132.44	5
1934-35	Did not play.					
1935-36	9	-	369	1,173	130.33	4
1936-37	19	1	270	1,552	86.22	6
1937-38	18	2	246	1,437	89.81	7
1938-39	7	1	225	919	153.16	6
1939-40	15	3	267	1,475	122.91	5
1940-41	4	-	12	18	4.50	0
1945-46	3	1	112	232	116.00	1
1946-47	14	1	234	1,032	79.38	4
1947-48	12	2	201	1,296	129.60	8
1948-49	4	-	123	216	54.00	1

IN ENGLAND

1930	36	6	334	2,960	98.66	10
1934	27	3	304	2,020	84.16	7
1938	26	5	278	2,429	115.66	13
1948	31	4	187	2,428	89.92	11
TOTAL	338	43	452*	28,067	95.14	117

IN TEST CRICKET

Opponents	Innings	Not Out	Highest Score	Runs	Average	Centuries
England	63	7	334	5,028	89.78	19
West Indies	6	-	223	447	74.50	2
South Africa	5	1	299*	806	201.50	4
India	6	2	201	715	178.75	4
TOTAL	80	10	334	6,996	99.94	29

* Not Out

NATURE OF BRADMAN'S DISMISSALS

	First class matches	All matches
Bowled	78	148
Caught by fieldsman	121	340 (caught, all types)
Caught and bowled	12	
Caught by wicketkeeper	40	
Stumped	12	22
Run out	4	14
Leg before wicket	27	37
Hit wicket	1	1
Not out	45	107
Total innings	338	669

RECORD SEASON BY SEASON

MATCH	FIRST INNINGS		SECOND INNINGS	
1927-1928 (In Australia)				
New South Wales v South Australia	c. Williams b. Scott	118	b. Grimmett	33
New South Wales v Victoria	l.b.w., b. Hartkoph	31	b. Blackie	5
New South Wales v Queensland	b. Gough	0	c. O'Connor, b. Nothling	13
New South Wales v South Australia	c. and b. McKay	2	st. Hack, b. Grimmett	73
New South Wales v Victoria	st. Ellis, b. Blackie	7	not out	134
1928-1929 (In Australia)				
New South Wales v MCC	b. Freeman	87	not out	132
An Australian X1 v MCC	not out	58	l.b.w., b. Tate	18
Australia v England (1st Test)	l.b.w., b Tate	18	c. Chapman, b. White	1
Australia v England (3rd Test)	b. Hammond	79	c. Duckworth, b. Geary	112
Australia v England (4th Test)	c. Larwood, b. Tate	40	run out	58
Australia v England (5th Test)	c. Tate, b. Geary	123	not out	37
New South Wales v MCC	c. Tyldesley, b.White	15		
The Rest v Australia	c. Oldfield, b.Grimmett	14	b. Oxenham	5
New South Wales v Queensland	c. O'Connor, b. Thurlow	131	not out	133
New South Wales v Victoria	b. Hendry	1	not out	71
New South Wales v South Australia	c. Grimmett, b. Wall	5	b. Wall	2
New South Wales v Victoria	not out	340		
New South Wales v South Australia	c. Walker, b. Grimmett	35	c.Walker, b. Carlton	175
1929-1930 (In Australia)				
New South Wales v MCC	b.Worthington	157		
Trial match	c. Jackson, b.Oxenham	124	l.b.w., b. Grimmett	225
New South Wales v Queensland	run out	48	c. O'Connor, b.Brew	66
New South Wales v South Australia	run out	2	l.b.w., b. Grimmett	84
New South Wales v Victoria	b. Alexander	89	not out	26
New South Wales v Queensland	c. Leeson, b.Hurwood	3	not out	452
New South Wales v South Australia	c. Richardson, b.Whitfield	47		
New South Wales v Victoria	ct. Ellis, b. Ironmonger	77		
1930 Australian X1 v Tasmania	l.b.w., b. Nash	20		
1930 Australian X1 v Tasmania	c. Rushforth, b. Atkinson	139		
1930 Australian X1 v Western Aust.	c. R.Bryant, b. Evans	27		
1930 (In England)				
Australians v Worcestershire	c.Walters, b. Brook	236		
Australians v Leicestershire	not out	185		
Australians v Yorkshire	c. and b. Macauley	78		
Australians v Lancashire	b. McDonald	9	not out	48
Australians v MCC	b. Allom	66	l.b.w., b. Stevens	4
Australians v Derby	c. Elliott, b. Worthington	44		
Australians v Surrey	not out	252		
Australians v Oxford University	b. Garland-Wells	32		
Australians v Hampshire	c. Mead, b. Boyes	191		
Australians v Middlesex	b. Hearne	35	b. Stevens	18
Australians v Cambridge University	c. Barnes, b. Human	32		
Australia v England (1st Test)	b. Tate	8	b. Robins	131
Australians v Surrey	c. Allom, b. Shepherd	5		
Australians v Lancashire	c. Duckworth, b. Sibbles	38	not out	23
Australia v England (2nd test)	c. Chapman, b. White	254	c. Chapman, b. Tate	1
Australians v Yorkshire	l.b.w., b. Robinson	1		
Australia v England (3rd Test)	c. Duckworth, b.Tate	334		
Australia v England (4th Test)	c. Duleepsinhji, b. Peebles	14		
Australians v Somerset	c. and b. Young	117		
Australians v Glamorgan	b. Ryan	58	not out	19
Australians v Northants	b. Jupp	22	c. Hawtin, b. Cox	35
Australia v England (5th Test)	c. Duckworth, b. Larwood	232		
Australians v Gloucestershire	c. Sinfield, b. Parker	42	b. Parker	14
Australians v Kent	l.b.w., b. Freeman	18	not out	205
Australians v An England X1	l.b.w., b. Allom	63		
Australians v Leveson-Gower's X1	b. Parker	96		

1930-1931 (In Australia)

Match	1st innings		2nd innings	
New South Wales v West Indians	c.Barrow, b. Francis	73	c. Headley, b. Martin	22
New South Wales v West Indians	b. Constantine	10	l.b.w., b. Griffith	73
Australia v West Indies (1st Test)	c. Grant, b.Griffith	4		
Australia v West Indies (2nd Test)	c. Barrow, b. Francis	25		
Australia v West Indies (3rd Test)	c. Grant, b. Constantine	223		
Australia v West Indies (4th Test)	c. Roach, b. Martin	152		
Australia v West Indies (5th Test)	c. Francis, b. Martin	43		
New South Wales v South Australia	c. Pritchard, b. Deverson	61	c. Waite, b. Deverson	121
New South Wales v South Australia	b. Richardson	258		
New South Wales v Victoria	c. Hendry, b. a'Beckett	2		
New South Wales v Victoria	c. Barnett, b. Alexander	55	c. Rigg, b. Ironmonger	220
Woodfull's X1 v Ryder X1	b. Mailey	73	c. and b. Mailey	29

1931-1932 (In Australia)

Match	1st innings		2nd innings	
New South Wales v South Africans	c. and b. McMillan	30	c. Bell, b. Morkel	135
New South Wales v South Africans	c. Curnow, b. McMillan	219		
New South Wales v Queensland	c. Waterman, b. Gilbert	0		
New South Wales v Victoria	c. Smith, b. Ironmonger	23	b. Nagel	167
New South Wales v South Australia	b. Carlton	23	b. Wall	0
Australia v South Africa (1st Test)	l.b.w., b. Vincent	226		
Australia v South Africa (2nd Test)	c. Viljoen, b. Morkel	112		
Australia v South Africa (3rd Test)	c. Cameron, b. Quinn	2	l.b.w., b. Vincent	167
Australia v South Africa (4th Test)	not out	299		

1932-1933 (In Australia)

Match	1st innings		2nd innings	
Combined X1 v MCC	c. Hammond, b. Verity	3	c. Pataudi, b. Allen	10
An Australian X1 v MCC	l.b.w., b. Larwood	36	b. Larwood	13
New South Wales v MCC	l.b.w., b. Tate	18	b. Voce	23
Australia v England (2nd Test)	b. Bowes	0	not out	103
Australia v England (3rd Test)	c. Allen, b. Larwood	8	c. and b. Verity	66
Australia v England (4th Test)	b. Larwood	76	c. Mitchell, b. Larwood	24
Australia v England (5th Test)	b. Larwood	48	b. Verity	71
New South Wales v MCC	b. Mitchell	1	c. Ames, b. Hammond	71
New South Wales v Victoria	c. O'Brien, b. Fleetwood-Smith	238	not out	52
New South Wales v Victoria	c. Bromley, b. Ironmonger	157		
New South Wales v South Australia	c. Ryan, b. Wall	56	b. Lee	97

1933-1934 (In Australia)

Match	1st innings		2nd innings	
New South Wales v Queensland	c. Andrews, b. Levy	200		
New South Wales v South Australia	b. Collins	1	st. Walker, b. Grimmett	76
New South Wales v Victoria	not out	187	not out	77
New South Wales v Queensland	b. Brew	253		
New South Wales v Victoria	c. Darling, b. Fleetwood-Smith	128		
Testimonial Match	c. Woodfull, b. Wall	55	c. Darling, b. Blackie	-101
New South Wales v The Rest	c. Walker, b. Chilvers	22	b. Ebeling	92

1934 (In England)

Match	1st innings		2nd innings	
Australians v Worcestershire	b. Howarth	206		
Australians v Leicestershire	b. Geary	65		
Australians v Cambridge University	b. Davies	0		
Australians v MCC	c. and b. Brown	5		
Australians v Oxford University	l.b.w., b. Dyson	37		
Australians v Hampshire	c. Mead, b. Baring	0		
Australians v Middlesex	c. Hulme, b. Peebles	160		
Australians v Surrey	c. Squires, b. Gover	77		
Australia v England (1st Test)	c. Hammond, b. Geary	29	c. Ames, b. Farnes	25
Australia v England (2nd Test)	c. and b. Verity	36	c. Ames, b. Verity	13
Australians v Northants	c. Bakewell, b. Mathews	65	b. Mathews	25
Australians v Somerset	c. Luckes, b. White	17		
Australians v Surrey	c. Brooks, b. Holmes	27	not out	61
Australia v England (3rd Test)	c. Ames, b. Hammond	30		
Australians v Derby	c. Elliott, b. Townsend	71	not out	6
Australians v Yorkshire	b. Leyland	140		
Australia v England (4th Test)	b. Bowes	304		
Australia v England (5th Test)	c. Ames, b. Bowes	244	b. Bowes	77
Australians v Essex	b. Pearce	19		
Australians v An English X1	not out	149		
Australians v Leveson-Gower's X1	st. Duckworth, b. Verity	132		

1935-1936 (In Australia)

Match	1st innings		2nd innings	
South Australia v MCC	l.b.w., b. Sims	15	l.b.w., b. Parks	50
South Australia v New South Wales	c. and b. Robinson	117		
South Australia v Queensland	c. Tallon, b.Levy	233		
South Australia v Victoria	c. Quin, b. Bromley	357		
South Australia v Queensland	c. Wyeth, b. Gilbert	31		
South Australia v New South Wales	c. Little, b. Hynes	0		
South Australia v Tasmania	c. and b. Townley	369		
South Australia v Victoria	c. Ledward, b. Ebeling	1		

1936-1937 (In Australia)

Match	1st innings		2nd innings	
An Australian X1 v MCC	b. Worthington	63		
Australia v England (1st Test)	c. Worthington, b. Voce	38	c. Fagg, b. Allen	0
Australia v England (2nd Test)	c. Allen, b. Voce	0	b. Verity	82
Australia v England (3rd Test)	c. Robins, b. Verity	13	c. Allen, b. Verity	270
South Australia v MCC	c. Ames, b. Barnett	38		
Australia v England (4th Test)	b. Allen	26	c. and b. Hammond	212
Australia v England (5th Test)	b. Farnes	169		
South Australia v Victoria	c. O'Brien, b. Gregory	192		
South Australia v Queensland	st. Tallon, b. Wyeth	123		
South Australia v New South Wales	l.b.w., b. O'Reilly	24	not out	38
South Australia v Victoria	c. Ebeling, b. Fleetwood-Smith	31	c. Hassett, b. McCormick	8
Testimonial Match	c. O'Reilly, b. Grimmett	212	c. Fingleton, b. Grimmett	15

1937-1938 (In Australia)

Match	1st innings		2nd innings	
South Australia v New South Wales	c. O'Brien, b. O'Reilly	91	c. Chipperfield, b. O'Reilly	62
South Australia v Queensland	c. Baker, b. Dixon	246	not out	39
South Australia v Victoria	c. Sievers, b. Gregory	54	c. Sievers, b. Gregory	55
South Australia v Queensland	c. Tallon, b. Dixon	107	c. Hackett, b. Allen	115
South Australia v New South Wales	c. McCabe, b. O'Brien	44	not out	104
South Australia v Victoria	b. McCormick	5	c. Ledward, b. Thorn	85
Testimonial Match	b. Grimmett	17		
South Australia v Western Australia	c. Wilberforce, b. Eyres	101		
South Australia v New Zealanders	c. Tindill, b. Cowie	11		
1938 Australian X1 v Tasmania	c. Sankey, b. Thomas	79		
1938 Australian X1 v Tasmania	b. Jeffrey	144		
1938 Australian X1 v Western Aust.	st. Lovelock, b. Zimbulis	102		

1938 (In England)

Australians v Worcestersire	c. Martin, b. Howarth	258		
Australians v Oxford University	l.b.w., b. Evans	58		
Australians v Cambridge University	c. Mann, b. Wild	137		
Australians v MCC	c. Robins, b. Smith	278		
Australians v Northants	c. James, b. Partridge	2		
Australians v Surrey	c. Brooks, b. Watts	143		
Australians v Hampshire	not out	145		
Australians v Middlesex	c. Compton, b. Nevell	5	not out	30
Australia v England (1st Test)	c. Ames, b. Sinfield	51	not out	144
Australians v Gentlemen	c. Valentine, b. Meyer	104		
Australians v Lancashire	c. Pollard, b. Phillipson	12	not out	101
Australia v England (2nd Test)	b. Verity	18	not out	102
Australians v Yorkshire	st. Wood, b. Smailes	59	c. Barber, b. Smailes	42
Australians v Warwickshire	c. Wilmot, b. Mayer	135		
Australians v Notts	l.b.w., b. Jepson	56	c. Jepson, b. Marshall	144
Australia v England (4th Test)	b. Bowes	103	c. Verity, b. Wright	16
Australians v Somerset	b. Andrews	202		
Australians v Glamorgan	st. H. Davies, b. Clay	17		
Australians v Kent	c. Todd, b. Watt	67		

1938-1939 (In Australia)

MCC Centenary Match	b. Nagel	118		
South Australia v New South Wales	b. Murphy	143		
South Australia v Queensland	c. Baker, b. Christ	225		
South Australia v Victoria	c. Hassett, b. Sievers	107		
South Australia v Queensland	c. Christ, b. W. Tallon	186		
South Australia v New South Wales	not out	135		
South Australia v Victoria	c. Fleetwood-Smith, b. Thorn	5		

1939-1940 (In Australia)

South Australia v Victoria	run out	76	l.b.w., b. Ring	64
South Australia v New South Wales	not out	251	not out	90
South Australia v Queensland	c. Hansen, b. Ellis	138		
South Australia v Victoria	c. Johnson, b. Fleetwood-Smith	267		
South Australia v Queensland	c. Dixon, b. Stackpole	0	c. Tallon, b. Cook	97
South Australia v New South Wales	l.b.w., b. O'Reilly	59	c. sub. b. Pepper	40
South Australia v Western Australia	c. Lovelock, b. MacGill	42	not out	209
South Australia v Western Australia	c. Zimbulis, b. Eyres	135		
Rest of Australia v New South Wales	c. Saggers, b. O'Reilly	25	c. McCool, b. Cheetham	2

1940-1941 (In Australia)

South Australia v Victoria	c. Sievers, b. Dudley	0	b. Sievers	6
Patriotic Match	c. Tamblyn, b. Ellis	0	b. O'Reilly	12

1945-1946 (In Australia)

South Australia v Queensland	c. Tallon, b. McCool	68	not out	52
South Australia v Services Team	c. Carmody, b. Williams	112		

1946-1947 (In Australia)

South Australia v MCC	c. and b. Smith	76	c. Edrich, b. Pollard	5
An Australian X1 v MCC	c. Pollard, b. Compton	106		
South Australia v Victoria	st. Baker, b. Johnson	43	st. Baker, b. Tribe	119
Australia v England (1st Test)	b. Edrich	187		
Australia v England (2nd Test)	l.b.w., b. Yardley	234		
Australia v England (3rd Test)	b. Yardley	79	c. and b. Yardley	49
Australia v England (4th Test)	b. Bedser	0	not out	56
Australia v England (5th Test)	b. Wright	12	c. Compton, b. Bedser	63
South Australia v MCC	c. Langridge, b. Wright	5		

1947-1948 (In Australia)

South Australia v Indians	c. Sarwate, b. Mankad	156	st. Sen, b. Mankad	12
South Australia v Victoria	l.b.w., b. Johnson	100		
An Australian X1 v Indians	c. Amarnath, b. Hazare	172	c. Sarwate, b. Mankad	36
Australia v India (1st Test)	hit wicket, b. Amarnath	185		
Australia v India (2nd Test)	b. Hazare	13		
Australia v India (3rd Test)	l.b.w., b. Phadkar	132	not out	127
Australia v India (4th Test)	b. Hazare	201		
Australia v India (5th Test)	retired hurt	57		
1948 Australian X1 v Western Aust.	c. Outridge, b. O'Dwyer	115		

1948 (In England)

Australians v Worcester	b. Jackson	107		
Australians v Leicester	c. Corrall, b. Etherington	81		
Australians v Surrey	b. Bedser	146		
Australians v Essex	b. P.Smith	187		
Australians v MCC	c. Edrich, b. Deighton	98		
Australians v Lancashire	b. Hilton	11	st. E. Edrich, b. Hilton	43
Australians v Notts.	b. Woodhead	86		
Australians v Sussex	b. Cornford	109		
Australia v England (1st Test)	c. Hutton, b. Bedser	138	c. Hutton, b. Bedser	0
Australians v Yorkshire	c. Yardley, b. Wardle	54	c. Hutton, b. Aspinall	86
Australia v England (2nd Test)	c. Hutton, b. Bedser	38	c. Edrich, b. Bedser	89
Australians v Surrey	c. Barton, b. Squires	128		
Australia v England (3rd Test)	l.b.w., b. Pollard	7	not out	30
Australians v Middlesex	c. Compton, b. Whitcombe	6	not out	173
Australia v England (4th Test)	b. Pollard	33		
Australians v Derby	b. Gothard	62		
Australians v Warwickshire	b. Hollies	31	not out	13
Australians v Lancashire	c. Wilson, b. Roberts	28	not out	133
Australia v England (5th Test)	b. Hollies	0		
Australians v Kent	c. Valentine, b. Crush	65		
Australians v Gentlemen	c. Donnelly, b. Brown	150		
Australians v South of England	c. Mann, b. Bailey	143		
Australians v Leveson-Gower's X1	c. Hutton, b. Bedser	153		

1948-1949 (In Australia)

Bradman Testimonial	c. Harvey, b. Dooland	123	c. Saggers, b. Johnston	10
Oldfield-Kippax Testimonial	c. Meuleman, b. Miller	53		
South Australia v Victoria	b. W. Johnston	30		

SUNDRIES

Rate of scoring: Bradman adapted his scoring rate to the state of the game. His average time to score 100 runs was 2 hours 46 minutes. His average time to move from 100 to 200 was 2 hours 18 minutes. On tour in England he scored centuries on each of 18 English grounds. At Leeds, he batted six times, averaging 192.60. At The Oval, he batted 12 times for an average of 139.20. Throughout his career, Bradman scored 42 runs an hour.

Sixes: Bradman's preference for keeping the ball on the ground, is indicated by the fact he hit only 46 sixes in his first-class career, most of these late in an innings when the state of the game dictated that he could do so.

Sheffield Shield: Bradman played in 62 Sheffield Shield matches between 1927 and 1949, 31 for NSW and the same number for South Australia. For NSW he averaged 107.74 and for South Australia 112.97.

Test matches: In Test matches be batted 80 times. In 51 of these, he scored less than 100, averaging 34. In the other 29 he exceeded 100 and averaged 234. In Tests, Bradman scored 25.47 per cent of his side's runs. The average runs added in Tests while Bradman was at the crease was 154, of which he scored 56 per cent.

Partnerships: Bradman shared 41 partnerships of 200 runs or more and 164 partnerships of 100 or more.

Centuries: He scored 117 first-class centuries, 29 of them in Tests. In 1938, he scored 13 on the tour of England. On three or more occasions he scored three or more centuries in a Test series. Hobbs did this twice. On two occasions, he scored centuries in three successive Tests against England. He scored numerous first-class centuries at better than a run-a-minute, including 101 not out in 73 minutes for the Australians versus Lancashire in 1938. He hit 15 fours. His fastest ever 100 was in a second-class match at Blackheath, NSW, in 1931. He scored the runs off 22 balls in three eight-ball overs. The time was thought to be less than 18 minutes.

Above left to right: Bradman 1974, 1948, 1930.

Index

PHOTOGRAPH CREDITS

Photographs in this book have been obtained from a wide variety of sources. The principal source has been the 51 volumes of Sir Donald Bradman's personal scrapbooks, compiled by the State Library of South Australia. Other photographs have come from John Fairfax Group Pty. Ltd., Sydney; *The Age*, Melbourne; The *Herald-Sun*, Melbourne; *The Advertiser*, Adelaide; *The Courier Mail*, Brisbane; News Ltd., Sydney; *The West Australian*, Perth; Sir Donald Bradman's private collection; friends of Sir Donald; The Bradman Museum, Bowral; the NSW Cricket Association; The State Library of NSW's At Work and At Play collection; The National Library of Australia, Canberra; C.R. Yeomans; Garry Edwards [front colour]; the Mailey family; the Jack Pollard collection; Joan Springett; Patrick Eagar; All-Sport, London; Keystone Collection, UK; BBC Hulton Picture Library; George Beldham Collection; and Happy Medium Photo Co., Warrandyte and numerous news agencies, including: Australian Associated Press; Associated Press; Sport and General, London; Central Press; World Wide Photos; Associated Newspapers; Photographic News Agencies; and Pacific and Atlantic Photos.

Every endeavour has been made to contact copyright owners, although in some cases it has been difficult to trace the origin of photographs because they carried no accreditation. Wherever possible, the owners have been contacted and permission obtained for reproduction. Should any person feel that illustrations, text or photographs, have been used without proper authority, he or she is invited to contact the publishers.

Acknowledgements

The co-publishers and editors gratefully acknowledge the assistance of a large number of people in the production of *Images of Bradman*. The material for the book has come from various sources, the principal one, Sir Donald Bradman's official scrapbooks, a 51-volume set. The originals are in the State Library of South Australia. Sir Donald's personal, duplicate set, is held by the National Library of Australia, Canberra.

The following books were of great assistance in providing quotations, statistics, photographic sources and supporting detail: *Farewell to Cricket*, D.G. Bradman [Hodder and Stoughton, London, 1950]; *Don Bradman's Book*, D.G. Bradman [Hutchison, London, 1950]; *The Bradman Albums*, Mortlock Library, Adelaide; *The Bradman Albums* [Weldons Pty. Ltd., Sydney, 1987]; *Bradman*, A.G. Moyes [Angus & Robertson, Sydney, 1948]; *Bradman, The Illustrated Biography*, Michael Page [The Macmillan Company of Aust. Pty. Ltd., 1983]; *Our Don Bradman*, Phillip Derriman [The Macmillan Company of Australia Pty. Ltd., 1987]; *Bodyline*, Phillip Derriman [William Collins Ltd., Sydney, 1984]; *Behind the Wickets*, W.A. Oldfield [Hutchison and Co., 1938]; *The Game Is Not The Same*, Alan McGilvrary with Norman Tasker [ABC Enterprises, 1985]; *Tiger*, Bill O'Reilly and edited Jack Egan [William Collins Pty. Ltd., Sydney, 1985]; *The Bradman Era*, Bill O'Reilly and complied by Jack Egan [ABC and William Collins Pty. Ltd., Sydney, 1983]; *The Pictorial History of Cricket*, Ashley Brown [Bison Books, London, 1988]; *It Isn't Cricket*, Sid Barnes [William Collins Ltd., 1953]; *A History of Cricket*, Benny Green [Guild Publishing, London, 1988]; *Brightly Fades The Don*, J.H. Fingleton [Collins, London, 1949]; *The Wisden Illustrated History of Cricket*, Vic Marks [Angus & Robertson, 1988]; *Flying Stumps*, Ray Lindwall [Stanley Paul and Co. Ltd., 1954]; *Cricket Crossfire*, Keith Miller [Oldbourne Press, 1950]; *Pageant of Cricket*, David Frith [Macmillan, Aust., 1987]; *The Larwood Story*, Harold Larwood, with Kevin Perkins [Bonpara Pty. Ltd., Sydney, 1982]; *Cardus In The Covers*, Neville Cardus [Souvenir Press, London, 1978]; *The Centurions*, Patrick Murphy [J.M. Dent and Sons Ltd., 1983]; *On Top Down Under, Australia's Cricket Captains*, Ray Robinson [Cassell Australia,1975]; *Sir Donald Bradman, A Biography*, Irving Rosenwater [Anchor Press Ltd., 1978]; *The Bradman Years*, *Australian Cricket, 1918-1948*, by Jack Pollard [Angus & Robertson Publishers, 1988], and *From Bradman to Border, Australian Cricket 1948-1989*, by Jack Pollard [Angus & Robertson Publishers, 1990].

The publishers greatly appreciate Sir Donald and Lady Bradman's assistance, also that of the Director of the Bradman Museum, Richard Mulvaney and his staff. Our thanks also to Richie Benaud, who wrote the foreword, and Tony Stephens, Assistant Editor of *The Sydney Morning Herald*, for his contribution, *Bradman-The Man and the Legend*.

Individual thanks go to numerous other people who assisted with this publication in various ways: Rose Toohey, Andrew Foulds, James Cottam, Lesley Mallet and Fortune Collict from John Fairfax Group Pty Ltd.; Darryl Newton; The Bradman Museum Trustees; Bob Radford, Chief Executive of the NSWCA; Heather Kelly, the NSWCA; the NSWCA photographic librarian, Steve Gibbs; John Benaud; Tony Greig; Lionel Marz, of Griffin Press; Esad Suskic of Prestige Colour; Max Suich; Sue Linsen; Ian Crowther; Ray Fuller; Tony Catts; Don Walker; Bill Brown; Keith Miller; Arthur Morris; Sam Loxton; Ernie Toshack; Ray Lindwall; Margaret Hughes, London; Joan Springett; Denis Compton; Alec Bedser; David Frith, Editor of *Wisden Cricket Monthly*; Gary Allen; Mike Morgan; Gordon and Mandy Foster; Jack Pollard; Jimera Pty. Ltd.; Blackheath Bowling Club; Elsie Thomas and Nancy Smith, of Blackheath; the staff of The National Library of Australia, Canberra; and Neil Thomas and his assistants at the State Library of South Australia, who spent many hours preparing photographic material.

Our special thanks to Steve Jones of Highland Graphics for all his hard work and to his wife Helen and son Reece for their hospitality.

A special thanks also to our families for their help, encouragement and tolerance: Marlene, Trent and Caitlin Allen; Helen, Jed and Hywel Kemsley.

While this book honours Sir Donald Bradman, it also honours the memory of another lesser known Australian my father, Frederick Allen, who, like Sir Donald, preached the Gospel of cricket as a game of enjoyment and entertainment and a builder of character, integrity and goodwill.

Peter Allen,
Editor and Co-publisher, 1994.

ALLEN & KEMSLEY PUBLISHING
The Laurels, 66-68 The Old Hume Highway,
Welby, NSW, Australia 2575.

Designed by: Steve Jones, Bowral.
Text set in Lingwood Demi Bold, Medium and Regular, 11/14 and 10/15 pt.
Printed by: Griffin Press, Adelaide.
Film and separation by Prestige Colour Pty Limited, 7 West Street, North Sydney.

Images of Bradman.
First published by Allen & Kemsley Publishing 1994,
in association with The Bradman Museum.

Copyright © Peter Allen and James Kemsley

National Library of Australia Cataloguing-in-Publication data.

Images of Bradman

Bibliography.
Includes index.
ISBN 0 646 19907 2.
ISBN 0 646 18944 1 (deluxe limited edition)
ISBN 0 646 19906 4 (collector's edition)

1. Bradman, Donald, Sir, 1908 - Portraits. 2. Cricket players - Australia - Pictorial works. I. Allen, Peter, 1940 - II. Kemsley, James, 1948.

796.358092